3-15-55

NEW LIFE IN OLD LANDS

NEW LIFE
IN OLD LANDS

by Kathleen McLaughlin

NEW YORK · 1954

DODD, MEAD & COMPANY

Copyright 1954
By Kathleen McLaughlin

Library of Congress Catalog Card Number: 54-11230

Printed in the United States of America
By the Vail-Ballou Press, Inc., Binghamton, N. Y.

FOREWORD

IT IS good to know that a veteran UN reporter with the integrity and ability of Kathleen McLaughlin, of the *New York Times*, has written about the technical assistance programs of the United Nations. While not familiar with the whole text, I can say that technical assistance, by helping the people of the world to help themselves, stands as one of the most effective expenditures of the United States dollar through the United Nations. The results of these programs can make life worth while and freedom worth fighting for.

AMBASSADOR HENRY CABOT LODGE, JR.

INTRODUCTION

WHEN THE sun comes up over the East River, the shadow of the forty-story Secretariat building at the United Nations falls just short of a cluster of residential hotels in midtown Manhattan. In one of these on a simmering day last summer, Sam M. Keeny, director of the Asian regional office for UNICEF, was unpacking his bags after a long plane trip from Bangkok. A sturdy man with crisp graying hair and a poker face that belies an eternally buoyant spirit, he was making good progress when the arrival of a white-smocked maid bearing an armful of towels gave him pause.

The girl was in the mood to chat. How long would he be staying, she inquired, and was he in New York on business?

"Just for a couple of days," he explained. "I'm here for an executive board meeting of the United Nation's Children's Fund, over there at headquarters."

He gestured through the window at the monolith of steel and glass rising along the riverbank. The girl's eyes widened.

"Oh—so that's what that building is!" she trilled. "I've been wondering what they made over there. You see, I used to work in a factory, too."

Incredulously, Mr. Keeny pondered her comment. To a man who has devoted years to the service of children in many countries on behalf of the agency, it seemed incomprehensible that any New Yorker could be oblivious to the identity of that group of buildings along First Avenue.

A week later the maid's remark returned to his consciousness with redoubled impact. By that time he was in the Philippines en route back to Thailand, and had stopped off overnight as a guest of James McCall, resident representative of the United Nations Children's Fund in the islands.

"There's something going on tonight we mustn't miss, Sam, no matter how tired you are," his host informed him. "The Igorot are staging a rare revival of old tribal dances, in the costumes their ancestors wore, and it will be quite a spectacle. You'll never forget it, so come along—you can rest when you get back to Bangkok."

Thus it came about that later that evening Sam Keeny found himself in a mountain glen, fascinated by the glare of torches and the weaving patterns of a barbaric dance rite. The atmosphere, it seemed to him, pulsed with genuine menace. Headlights of automobiles parked at the edge of the clearing glowed redly with the reflected flames of brush fires about which these modern Igorots writhed and circled. Garish colors daubed their bodies. Their voices rose chillingly in the hysterical chants that once set their forbears on the warpath. Spectators felt their flesh prickling at the ferocity with which they brandished their clubs and spears.

The man from Bangkok could hardly wrest his eyes from one huge native, so intimidating in appearance and so threatening of manner that he might well have reverted utterly to type. Uneasily, Sam wondered how near to the real thing this playacting might go.

But the drumming and the dancing ceased, and a reassuring quiet fell. Then the visitor glimpsed his host emerging through the gloom, shepherding the same formidable figure on which his whole attention had been riveted.

"Sam, I want you to meet the mayor," he heard. With a wide smile, the big Igorot put out his hand in greeting. His voice was warm and cultured, his English flawless.

"Mr. McCall tells me you are a United Nations man, too," the Filipino said.

"Yes. I work in Bangkok," Mr. Keeny acknowledged, still a bit bemused. "I'm with the Children's Fund."

"UNICEF!" boomed the pseudosavage, delightedly. "Why—I know it very well. In fact, I'm in charge of the distribution of UNICEF milk to all the children in this area. We are very glad to welcome you, sir!"

Somewhat dazed, Mr. Keeny permitted himself to be ushered back to the car that had brought him to the scene.

On the drive back to Manila, his companion remarked, "You've been awfully quiet, Sam. What are you thinking so hard about?"

Sam roused himself.

"About how paradoxical it is," he retorted, "that people in parts of the world like this understand and appreciate the work of the United Nations so much more clearly than the average man or woman in what we call advanced countries. Let me tell you about a maid in my hotel in New York. . . ."

Somewhere between these two extremes of reaction lies the normal response of the world public to the United Nations. The blithe unawareness of the maid who thought its façade concealed merely another water-front factory is hardly typical. Neither, on the other hand, was the intimate knowledge displayed by Sam's Igorot acquaintance. Despite distance, this man had been opportunely situated to see staff personnel of the world organization actually at work. The erstwhile factory girl had missed such proximity. Even though her job placed her close enough to shy a pebble into the headquarters fountain, and she had caught mention of the United Nations in conversation and on radio programs to which she listened daily, she had not located its site and had never heard of UNICEF. Most literate people are considerably better informed than the New Yorker of this anecdote, but rather less familiar with the UN and its works than the Igorot.

The explanation is simple. In countries blessed with adequate telecommunications, attention has focused on such significant developments as the vote in the Security Council against aggression in Korea; the armistice negotiations in Kashmir, Palestine or Indonesia; or the debates in the General Assembly on disarmament, including control of the atom bomb.

In blighted or underdeveloped areas where telephones and telegraph lines are rare and television quite unknown, it is a different countenance that the United Nations turns toward the populations. There, international clashes are vague and remote, arousing only minor interest. Even wars become important only when they loom close on the home horizon.

People in these regions are too engrossed in the struggle for sheer existence, groping for a way out of the morass of poverty and illness that confronts them at every turn. Nowhere is the United Nations so literally and so helpfully a part of the daily routine.

Penetrate the hinterlands of any continent where the rice is sparse, the soil arid, the population quaking with malaria or housing the most miserable, and sooner or later you will cross the trail of United Nations teams administering some facet of its Technical Assistance program. There the field-workers labor, not in the striped trousers of diplomacy but in the dusty corduroys and windbreakers, the well-worn dungarees or the much-laundered uniforms of clinicians energetically on the job. There the United Nations is a living, active entity.

In backward little settlements all over the globe, hundreds of thousands of men, women and children can explain to whoever asks, that the United Nations works in partnership with their own governments; that its representatives are there to help them raise more crops, extend their roads and banish epidemics. They will report with conscious gratification that their country pays for much of this help, but that the experts who live and work with them are sent by several agencies, through the United Nations.

Glibly they will tick off the familiar initials of the units they happen to know best. If theirs has been a particularly distressed land, they are apt to know quite a few.

Deep in the African bush country, for example, lives a keenly intelligent, wholly illiterate chieftain in his middle years, who has never heard of Korea or Kashmir. But he knows UNESCO well. For its representatives taught one of his more promising young men to read and write and to use a typewriter. With the aid of this newly acquired secretary, the chief dictated a letter to the provincial governor, asking for help in fulfilling his ambition of years—to build a road from his territory to the nearest large town. He knew that it would mean the end of isolation for his people, and a market for their produce.

More than a year ago the road, twenty-eight miles long, was finished. For the tribe it has proved a bridge to a new kind of life. For their farsighted leader, it has not been an end, but a beginning—of other dreams.

In northern Burma, in the mountain fastnesses to which they retreated across the border of their homeland when victorious Communist troops overran it years ago, guerrilla warfare has been waged ever since by a remnant of the Chinese Nationalist forces. Between raids to harass the foe to the east, these warlords have badgered their unwilling hosts, the Burmese. Yet when word was passed to them that World Health teams were in the vicinity and would come to dust the houses and the population with DDT against malaria if they would agree to suspend operations for that interval, the pledge was not only given, but scrupulously kept. Once the sprayings were completed and the medicos safely away, shooting began again!

Far up in the Peruvian highlands a weekly distribution of dried milk from UNICEF was in progress last year when a weary, unknown crew tied up a clumsy, native rowboat at the lake landing. The occupants, a bevy of Andean Indians that included a couple of mothers, shuffled forward to plead for a share of the supplies for their own children. Astonished, UNICEF workers asked questions. Where had they come from? How had they learned about this team and its routes? And how had they known its schedule, and been able to time their arrival so neatly?

While they rested from their exertions, the Indians supplied the answers. They lived many miles away, across the big lake and deep in the mountains beyond. Word of the UNICEF mission had been carried by mouth from one tiny village to another. Every detail had been spread about it, from the number of its personnel to the quantities of supplies they carried, and the time and place of each stop made on the weekly rounds. This journey, just completed, had required two days of travel by land and water. It had been undertaken as soon as they had been able to estimate where they might count on making this contact. They wanted that milk brought also to their region.

Milk they might have, and gladly, the tired group was assured. Unfortunately there was neither transport nor staff available, to get it to their distant neighborhood.

"Just count us in on the rations," they begged. "We will come ourselves and collect them. The children must have the milk—there is so little else for them, this year."

So it was arranged, and these resolute boatmen have made the grueling trip regularly. Week after week they have arrived at the rendezvous. They stow the fiberboard drums aboard their craft and struggle back with them across the lake and up the rocky pinnacles to their homes. On land they pack the loads after their traditional fashion, on their own backs, securing them with cloths bound around their own foreheads and also encircling the drums.

Their concept of the United Nations is different from that of newspaper readers in Council Bluffs, or Henley-on-Thames or Bordeaux, and essentially more intimate. They know UNICEF.

Mention the General Assembly or the Security Council in any of these countries, and only a handful will respond with other than blank looks. But bring up the WHO or the FAO or UNESCO, and the odds are good that there will be an answering flash of comprehension—recognition of an old friend. Often the connection between these agencies and the United Nations remains misty, in such company. Quite a few are utterly ignorant of the phrase "technical assistance." It matters little. What they do grasp is much more important—the friendliness of these foreigners among them, the surprising results they achieve, the horizons that are opened up through their patient teaching of the under-nourished, illiterate and unskilled populations. And not least, the fact that these technicians come to them through an association of nations in which their own has a voice and a vote.

Now discuss the TA with a run-of-the-mill, average American or European, and note how vague the reaction can be to the program that "has something to do with building dams or growing more food in poor countries—or isn't that it?"

Yet this is precisely the public that is paying for a considerable share of the work done by the Technical Assistance representatives. These basic contributions—through the taxes paid into their respective national treasuries—are helping to finance progress for the underprivileged, and to accomplish these changes at a rate they themselves only dimly realize.

The sheer vastness of the TA panorama, in fact, defeats any easy grasp of its scope. Though it has taken years as against Puck's forty minutes, the experts dispatched have managed to "put a girdle round about the earth." To scan more than a section of their assignments, either a world tour would be necessary, or an impossible vantage somewhere out in space, maintained for a full day's twirling of the globe on its axis.

A fog of noncomprehension therefore remains to be dispelled, bit by bit. One possible alternative is the one this book represents. Here is a compilation of vignettes from a number of countries, designed to convey enough of the variety, the drama, and some of the humor of the TA missions to suggest the pattern and the problems of all.

Its source is the fieldworkers who know best and tell best, the sights, sounds, smells, frustrations, philosophies, tragedies and triumphs of the people and the places encompassed in these pages. It is their story as they told it, in reports and in interviews mailed in from their far-flung stations, or delivered while they were comfortably ensconsed on the leather divans or behind a borrowed desk in the Secretariat building on First Avenue, availing themselves of a few brief hours of relaxation as they scooted through on leave, alert not to miss their planes back to Jakarta or Bali, Bogotá or Dakar.

This is their story of the TA work. If it helps to make more vivid the changes that are evolving so significantly, at a gradually increasing tempo year by year, it will have served.

CONTENTS

xvii

CONTENTS

xviii

ILLUSTRATIONS

Afghanistan farmers are taught by Dr. Martin Sommerauer, an FAO technician, the proper care of new tools to stimulate food production.

"Fish farming," centuries old in China, is being popularized in many countries, adding valuable proteins to deficient diets.

Vast numbers of Ethiopian cattle are being rescued from epidemics of rinderpest by vaccination.

Volunteer workers in Emporion, Greece, built their flood control dam by hand, in their spare time.

Underground water sources, located by surveys, are tapped for irrigation or for household use.

Running water comes to Loma de Ramas. The government contributed the pipes.

Togolanders are seeing the same UNESCO film-strip—on agriculture—they have seen nightly for three weeks past.

Bolivia has 2,000 lower schools, but only recently built one for these Indian boys at Caroica.

Word comes to the Quijano family that a new home in El Salvador's housing program has been reserved for them.

The Quijanos take possession of one of 250 tile-roofed brick houses in the Sitio del Niño project.

Scientists are aiding UNESCO in studying ways of reclaiming such arid land as this, in Africa.

(All photographs from the United Nations files)

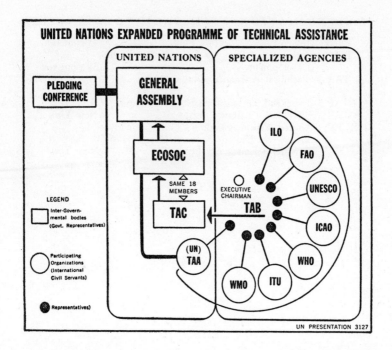

UNITED NATIONS EXPANDED PROGRAMME OF TECHNICAL ASSISTANCE

UNITED NATIONS   SPECIALIZED AGENCIES

PLEDGING CONFERENCE

GENERAL ASSEMBLY

ECOSOC

SAME 18 MEMBERS

TAC

EXECUTIVE CHAIRMAN

TAB

ILO
FAO
UNESCO
ICAO
WHO
ITU
WMO

(UN) TAA

LEGEND

Inter-Governmental bodies (Govt. Representatives)

Participating Organizations (International Civil Servants)

Representatives)

UN PRESENTATION 3127

All of the agencies participating in the program of aid to under-developed countries are linked through the Technical Assistance Board and the Technical Assistance Committee, to the Economic and Social Council, which in turn is responsible to the General Assembly, comprising sixty nations.

SPECIALIZED AGENCIES OF THE UNITED NATIONS

		Headquarters
ILO –	International Labor Organization	Geneva
FAO –	Food and Agriculture Organization	Rome
UNESCO –	United Nations Educational, Scientific and Cultural Organization	Paris
WHO –	World Health Organization	Geneva
ICAO –	International Civil Aviation Organization	Montreal
ITU –	International Telecommunication Union	Geneva
WMO –	World Meterological Organization	Lausanne
UPU –	Universal Postal Union	Bern

(Continued on next page)

xxi

UNITED NATIONS' SPECIALIZED AGENCIES

Fund	– International Monetary Fund	Washington
Bank	– International Bank for Reconstruction and Development	Washington
TAA	– Technical Assistance Administration	United Nations, New York
ETAP	– Expanded Technical Assistance Program	New York
TAB	– Technical Assistance Board	New York
UNICEP	– United Nations Children's Fund, formerly known as United Nations International Children's Emergency Fund	New York

NEW LIFE IN OLD LANDS

ONE

MODERN MAGIC

EL SALVADOR

WHEN THE station wagon reached the plaza in front of the church in Guazapa, its occupants found themselves surrounded by a milling crowd, and knew that they had come in time. It was not yet eight o'clock in the morning, and it was going to be a scorcher of a day. The people stood about, laughing and chatting in carnival mood, waiting for the mass to begin. Every few minutes an odd kind of rocket was touched off. Snaking upward, it would explode about 200 feet in the air with a fine, loud bang, sending tots diving to hide their heads in their mothers' skirts.

Piled neatly row on row near the church steps lay the utilitarian-looking water pipes that were the occasion for all this hubbub. Presently these celebrators would hoist them to their shoulders and step proudly out to carry them five miles further up, along a twisting mountain trail, to their own village of Loma de Ramas (Hill of the Branches). When they had been linked and cemented into place, life would be brighter and less rigorous for young and old.

Anticipation of the better times ahead had fired these El Salvadoreans. It had roused an entire community of 300

1

persons from bed at five o'clock, to come streaming down the mountain, shouting and cheering, to turn themselves temporarily into the pack mules they neither owned nor had money to hire, so that the precious pipes might reach their destination and begin their appointed service. No one was missing, from Señor Timo, the oldest inhabitant, to the tiniest—a three-months-old infant cradled in its mother's arms.

In more than a century of existence, Loma de Ramas had never known such a day. So why not make a *fiesta* of it?

Five New Yorkers in the station wagon, already briefed on the significance of the scene, spent only a few moments contemplating the stirring panorama. They had work to do. They leaped from their vehicle—courtesy of the government of El Salvador—and began unloading equipment.

Out came a tape recorder for sound, in charge of Emil Corwin. Next came still cameras, to be handled by Al Fox; motion-picture apparatus, which Bob Ziller would operate, with Brett Porter directing; and a reporter's notebook and pencils, with which Len Berry would preserve his impressions, and the names of participants. All were staff members from the United Nations headquarters on the East River. They were in Latin America on an extended field trip, recording in film and sound exactly this type of episode, about which they had heard just in time, only the previous day.

More enthusiastic than experienced, they planned to scramble up the mountain along with the crowd, shooting pictures and recording the gaiety and the color of it all as they went. This they did, in fact, although they almost foundered in the process. Thanks to their fortitude, they brought to life for the rest of us in more privileged parts of the world, the day-to-day activities of various agencies of the United Nations that have engaged in hundreds of such exploits. Their narrative has already been broadcast over national networks, and their film documentary is gradually gaining wide circulation.

In this instance it was the World Health Organization that planted the seed of the idea. Working in collaboration with the Health Bureau of El Salvador, WHO sanitary engineers had visited Loma de Ramas routinely, and had observed that the inhabitants were forced to carry all their water from a spring three kilometers (nearly two miles) above their town. There was no nearer source. Vessels used were earthen pitchers, balanced on their heads as they scrambled up, then down again. The round trip was necessary half a dozen times daily for each family, yet there was never enough water to keep themselves and their households clean.

When the engineers first suggested that the government might be willing to supply pipes to bring that spring water right down into their houses, the whole community was lifted up to the seventh heaven of expectation. The very idea that they might have tub baths and plenty of water for laundering turned them giddy with joy. They waited impatiently for developments. By the time their dream had neared realization through the delivery of the pipes in Guazapa, five miles below them on the trail and the closest accessible point, they could wait no longer.

Someone said, "We could bring them up, ourselves!"

From that moment, they knew that they would. Every living soul in Loma de Ramas must participate, even the babies.

Now here they all were. And there before them were their pipes—shining metal ones of aluminum-coated iron, twenty feet in length and about an inch in diameter; and sturdy concrete sections about three feet long and four inches across. The longer and narrower ones would bring down the water for their drinking, cooking and laundering. The larger ones would serve as drains. No longer would the boys and girls toil incessantly up and down, back and forth to the spring, day after day. They would have time to go to school, to help with household chores—even to play as other children did.

Bang! went the rockets. "Yiah!" yelped the little ones. From their twin steeples, the church bells pealed a summons.

Then the men took off their scoop-brimmed straw hats—their protection against the sun—and the women tossed bright cotton scarves over their dark hair, and they all went into the whitewashed church that looked so much like the Spanish mission chapels in California. The service of sanctification and of thanksgiving began.

Only a few minutes earlier Father Osmaro Alvarenga, the congenial pastor at Guazapa, had mischievously touched off the last of the rockets, while still in his black cassock and Panama hat. Now at the altar in priestly robes, he gave them a special sermon, interspersed with lightly humorous references to their expedition.

"I give you my enthusiastic congratulations," he said in Spanish, "inasmuch as very few villages attain the success which you are realizing. Before God who guides us, we know of the captivity in Egypt of the chosen people of Israel, and

4

of how the Pharaohs wanted to keep them there, in order to enslave and exploit them. And God gave them a brave and expert guide to take them out of their captivity and bring them to the Promised Land, where, as it had been foretold, they would enjoy a place of great prosperity and peace.

"Here you also find yourselves in exile. It is uncomfortable and difficult to climb up to where you live—somewhat barren places without even the public drinking water which is available to those living in the valley. You shall now have water, and those who have taken you out of the captivity of the scarcity of water are Dr. Sequeira and his assistants (of the WHO), that God has sent you."

"Amen!" murmured the people. Their responses rolled like music through the little church.

The mass was ended. Father Osmaro took off his colorful vestments, donned a lacy white surplice, and taking in one hand his missal and in the other the hyssop newly filled with holy water, went outside for the brief, solemn rite of blessing for the people and their piles of pipes. All stood hushed, the men with their hats in their hands. The moment it was over, they burst into lusty Spanish cheers, and the singing began again.

Before they could start away, the hospitable people of Guazapa rushed up to bid them come and have coffee at the town hall nearby. Soon they were all sipping the strong brew, but the interval was brief. Waving and calling their thanks to their hosts, they moved back to the church, the men adjusting on their shoulders the blankets they had brought to ease the weight of the iron pipes, and the women wadding their cotton scarves into pads atop their heads, where they

5

would balance the shorter, wider pipes.

By this time the temperature was hovering above ninety degrees, Fahrenheit, and inching steadily upward. Incredulously, the United Nations group surveyed the bare feet of the men, women and children—only a few wore shoes—and the rocky, boulder-strewn trail up which they were starting. Yet the only complaints they heard were from men whose pipes had not been decorated with the small blue paper flags that fluttered from most of the longer sections. El Salvadorean national colors are blue and white, inquiry brought out. The women had brought the tiny banners as a patriotic touch.

Soon the strangers were footsore and panting, scrambling for footholds on the trail. Abashed, they tried to keep up with the mountain people, who climbed easily with their heavy burdens, as sure of their footing as their own native goats. A lone mule had been obtained to carry the tape recorder and the film apparatus, and the men from New York grinned at one another in embarrassment at their relative helplessness. They tried to pry away from the children some of the shorter lengths of the concrete pipes, or to relieve some of the women who clasped a baby in one arm and a unit of pipe in the other. Not one could be found who would relinquish his trophy. Nor even for a part of the distance, would a native yield his role in the procession to an outsider! They merely laughed, waving aside all proffers of assistance.

At one point a wide, shallow creek flowed across the trail. The men paused before fording it, to roll up their trousers, then waded unconcernedly across its stony bottom. The women, with their short skirts reaching just below their knees, had no trouble keeping them dry. Just beyond this point the rough ground got rougher, as the people plodded on across clusters of large, sharp-surfaced rocks. The pace hardly slowed, as they stepped from one to another of these boulders with catlike grace.

About halfway up, a halt was called under a group of shade trees, and the United Nations men dropped thankfully to the ground, to enjoy the respite. They were acutely aware of thirst, and of their parched throats. Never had the boon of water seemed so wonderful to them, as the pitchers passed from hand to hand and they could take long gulps of even this tepid liquid. Many of the natives, they noted, were sucking limes instead, as they rested on a stone wall under the trees.

With time to look about them, Corwin and Berry and the others traded observations. All were amazed at the endurance of the women who balanced a pipe on one shoulder and a baby on the other, and amused at the strutting little seven-year-old boy who clasped in one arm the weighty kit of Al Fox's camera equipment. This little fellow stolidly smoked a stogie throughout most of the march.

Twice during the climb they rested. It was late afternoon when the picturesque procession filed into the town square at Loma de Ramas, and the triumphant people put down their pipes on home territory. Weary as they were, the welkin rang with their chanting and their cheers. The newcomers looked about at these humble dwellings and at the sturdy folk who lived there, and felt that the day was symbolic of the feats El Salvadoreans could perform in the future, with such help as their government was extending.

There, at close quarters, the strangers could appreciate more fully how great a change was impending through that new community water system. Most of the huts were fashioned of adobe and wood. Others were built of strong reeds, bound and interwoven together with twine, and topped with thatched roofs. The floors were merely packed mud. In several a large, unhewn stone in the center served as a rude sort of combination table and stove. Fires lighted there smoked unrestainedly, their smothering fumes finding outlets through the uncurtained doorways or between gaps in the walls.

Thanks to the consistently mild climate, the people here need no protection against snow or bitter weather, but in the rainy season that prevails about three months each year, life is acutely uncomfortable. Some homes are of mud packed with straw, and have a tendency to flake away under impact of a heavy downpour. Resultant holes are repaired when time permits.

As twilight fell that evening in Loma de Ramas, the shortcomings of their houses bothered the celebrators little. They clustered excitedly about Dr. Francisco Sequeira, health educator for the government and a frequent visitor to the community, who had accompanied them on their climb. Discussions went forward with him in rapid Spanish about the installation of the pipes, and he was plied with requests to pass on to the foreign guests, details about their lives or their villages. The United Nations reporters were eagerly receptive.

The villagers, they learned, cultivated beans, rice and

corn on their sloping fields, and raised hens and pigs. They even had a few cows. The Salvadorean authorities were sure that the new water system would improve their health, particularly that of the children. Later, perhaps, the diligent planning under way by the government in the housing field would bring them another type of aid. They might even eventually share in the educational system that is being extended—too slowly to satisfy their administration officials—to these hinterland areas.

For the present, Dr. Sequeira said, the mental horizon of these villagers was being widened through occasional films that are brought up to them, including documentaries on health subjects. They have already absorbed quite a few of the simple precautions recommended. The WHO nurses had persuaded them to boil all the water they drank or used for cooking, to reduce the risk of typhoid, and the natives brought out for exhibit the earthen pitchers in which they kept these safe reserves.

Lengthening shadows warned the United Nations team that they must be off. On the dark, unfamiliar trail, with only a single flashlight to guide their uncertain feet, they faced a renewed ordeal in groping their way back down to their vehicle. So they bowed out amid much handwaving and hearty if unintelligible wishes for a safe return journey, and trudged away, leaving the people to finish their celebration with a bit of dancing for those who still had the energy to lift their feet.

None of the five men from the north will ever forget that tedious trip back down the trail to Guazapa. Bone weary, they stumbled and slid and bumped themselves against boulders too tardily glimpsed in the rays of their feeble torch. Hours later, they had slogged it out and were creeping painfully back into their station wagon, groaning with exhaustion but protesting individually that they would "do it again for as good a story." In every mind glowed a livelier respect for the endurance of individual fieldworkers for United Nations agencies, to whom such difficulties are normal.

All through their roamings in El Salvador they sensed the vitality of the movement afoot to lift this tiny republic —the smallest in Central America—out of the sloughs in which it has struggled overlong. On its own, the government in 1933 had launched what seemed an admirable plan to parcel out land to needy farmers, hoping to make them independent. It also had made a heroic effort to provide adequate houses, as substitutes for their humble shacks. But its intentions were better than its procedures. The farmers needed more than land. They needed equipment, supplies of seed grain, advice about planting and fertilizing and help with their marketing. The government's funds did not stretch that far. Within a few years all the holdings ended up in the possession of a few wealthy landowners who had picked them up for a song. The peasants were forced to leave their government-built homes and go back to their original dwellings and their parched, unproductive earth.

This time the El Salvador government has acquired powerful allies for the projects it is launching, and prospects of success are considerably brighter.

In the last six years it has had invaluable help and

financial backing from the International Bank—which advanced a loan of $12,545,000 to probe the possibilities of the Lempa River Hydroelectric Scheme; from the United States, through its Point Four program; and from the United Nations, to which it turned for aid as early as 1947. The breadth of the ventures developing under United Nations auspices is indicated by the fact that they involve the International Labor Organization (ILO); the Food and Agriculture Organization (FAO); the Children's Fund (UNICEF); the United Nations Educational, Scientific and Cultural Organization (UNESCO); the International Civil Aviation Organization (ICAO), and the World Health Organization (WHO).

Lieutenant Colonel Oscar Osorio, president of El Salvador, has gladly acknowledged in his public pronouncements the value of the co-operation between his administration and the personnel of these varying units.

Out of this free interplay has arisen a living laboratory of almost unique interest to other nations. Known as the Cuscatlan Valley Demonstration Project, it represents a concerted attack on malnutrition, infant and maternal mortality, and illiteracy and poor sanitation, while stimulating agriculture, proper use of the soil, adequate housing, cottage crafts and the general welfare of the workers.

Cuscatlan lies almost directly in the center of the country. It was selected because its terrain embraces both mountains and valleys, making it typical of many districts in Latin America. It has a population of about 160,000, distributed among some fairly large towns, and many villages and hamlets. Volcanic peaks frown down upon fertile lowlands, waste lands, rivers, large plantations and small farms. Bougainvillaea in rich, deep shades clambers over fences and houses, and orchids grow wild. There are cottage industries but no sizable factories, and workshops specialize in hand weaving. Schools are inadequate both in number and in facilities, and attendance is consistently poor. In the municipality of Cuidad Arce, out of 2,700 children of school age, only 500 were registered in the two schools.

In this lovely valley, as in most of the more backward regions, the physical condition of the people was the most acute problem. UNICEF and WHO tackled it together. From the Children's Fund came supplies of DDT, and WHO—which had contracted to spend $150,000 here to provide technical personnel and supplies—sent in its teams to handle the routine dusting techniques as the battle against malaria began, in September 1951. The government's men kept step, learning as they went.

Three months later the entire demonstration area had been covered through the insect-control campaign. Approximately 17,500 houses had been entered and sprayed with DDT, protecting 105,000 persons against further infection. And three training courses had been set up, for graduate nurses, sanitary inspectors and auxiliary nurses.

UNICEF operations were merged, meanwhile, with the government's moves toward provision of school lunches. The start had been made in recognition of the extent of malnutrition among the pupils. One out of every three reporting to the clinics, it had been found, was suffering from acute "hunger sickness," and the youngsters were languid and apathetic toward lessons.

But when UNICEF made a commitment to supply skim milk for a major feeding demonstration, and the first powdered milk arrived in April 1950, protests were raised by the teachers. Overworked, discouraged and unfamiliar with the dehydrated milk, they complained that it was no better than flour, that they had no time to mix it with boiled water, and that in any case it did not taste good. Two months later the picture had changed. More than 32,000 children were happily drinking the milk and demanding more—and more. Opposition from the teachers evaporated as they began to report that their once listless charges were wide-awake, interested and learning much more rapidly.

The momentum quickened as this appreciation spread to parents, and then to local authorities. Requests began to pile up for additional information about nutrition. Mayors pulled strings to get UNICEF milk into their communities. The country had boasted only two clinics for infant nutrition, but sixty days after the first shipment of the powdered milk, fourteen community clinics were open and twenty-six more in preparation.

Within eighteen months subsequent to April 1950, UNICEF had expended $52,400 on the program, but had stimulated national and municipal expenditures of $276,-744—almost five to one.

In every angle of the health phase of the project, El Salvadorean health officials have been and are at the elbows of WHO and UNICEF fieldworkers. The international and the native teams joined forces as maternity- and child-health clinics were opened and Salvadorean women and girls were recruited to learn nursing and midwifery. BCG vaccine was brought in and the antituberculosis battle—always a long and discouraging routine—was started. Dental laboratories were set up, and found work in plenty.

The FAO was busy also, on a score of enterprises that could come to fruition only slowly. The Cuscatlan Valley soil is rated among the best in El Salvador, producing twelve per cent of the corn and forty-one per cent of the country's sugar crop. But due to the extremities of mountain and plain confronting them, the experts faced simultaneous problems of drainage and of irrigation. Destruction of forests has been responsible for a serious water shortage in the country. There was practically no understanding by the people of the meaning or importance of conservation, or of the necessity for efficient utilization of the soil. Technicians labored to spread among the farmers a knowledge of proper agricultural methods. Progress is not yet satisfactory, but advances continue.

For UNESCO, the Cuscatlan Valley posed a different type of challenge. Teachers as well as schools were scarce, and more of both were needed before school attendance could begin to show improvement. Two specialists in fundamental education and literacy techniques—one a Belgian, one a Mexican—were assigned by UNESCO to help the government reorganize the school system. They have completed the planning stage of their work, and the training of El Salvadorean teachers in fundamental education is under way.

ILO's part of the work has been directed toward encouraging the people to revive native handicrafts. It is planned gradually to open up markets for cottage industries, as they develop. Skills in this field not only help to increase family earnings, but also widen the interests and raise the morale of those who participate.

Neither the United Nations nor the government envisages in this experiment the creation of a "valley of privilege" in an underprivileged country. The site was chosen because it typified the assets and liabilities existing in several Latin American nations. Experience gained on this project can accelerate the successes and eliminate the failures of similar attempts to guide sick and unfortunate human beings into an independent and productive way of life.

The difficulties, especially on the health side, are enormous. The life expectancy of the average citizen is only twenty-six years. Forty per cent of the population are under fifteen, and only four per cent above sixty years of age. El Salvador is only 160 miles long and about sixty wide, and is considered the highest in density of population in the Western Hemisphere. The average income is less than $250 a year, and the people are subject to communicable diseases inevitably associated with malnutrition and poor sanitary conditions.

But good sanitation, if it is integrated with sound agricultural practices, can do much to improve the situation. K. K. Jensen of Denmark, a dairy consultant, was therefore imported by the FAO to study the whole question of dairy farming, to suggest ways and means of increasing milk production, and of achieving a better quality of milk.

As deliberate and as thorough as any of his countrymen, Mr. Jensen, before attacking his special mission, toured El Salvador, visiting all important facilities in his bailiwick.

He reported some very fine dairy farms, especially in the vicinity of Santa Anna, the second largest metropolis in the country. But there, he found, they owed their existence and their superiority to the coffee planters. The plantation owners wanted natural manure to increase their coffee yield. To insure a large enough supply, they had purchased thoroughbred cattle from the United States. The aristocratic bossies had been so well handled, housed and pastured that the quality of their milk was outstanding. These farms, however, were notable exceptions. Most of the dairy farms were small and ineptly operated.

The Dane quickly discovered his most enthusiastic backer in the minister of agriculture. This official was himself a cattleman and the owner of a fine farm near San Salvador. Mr. Jensen was cheered to learn from him that in collaboration with UNICEF, the government plans to build a plant to produce milk powder, for use in feeding programs for children.

On the debit side Mr. Jensen placed the low milk consumption in El Salvador—only one fifth of a liter per capita per day, as against the average of one liter per day in Europe and in the United States. (A liter equals 1.0537 quarts.) To encourage dairy farmers to maintain their output in winter as well as in summer, the Danish expert advised the government to stabilize the price of milk, so that the people would not stop drinking it as the cost advanced during colder weather.

He is also promoting the acceptance of rigid sanitation measures to improve the quality of milk throughout the country. This means "selling" the importance of sanitation to every individual dairyman. In lectures he has given at the School of Agriculture to governmental assistants, the FAO man has resorted to applied science to put over his points.

He produces a series of petri dishes—flat, shallow trays used in chemical laboratories. One of the dishes has been sterilized. On this he places a few drops of clean milk. Then he places a wisp of straw on one drop, captures a fly and lets it skitter through another. Presently, he invites the class to inspect under a microscope the colonies of bacteria that have formed around the straw, or the tracks left by the fly.

The demonstration is usually convincing, but Mr. Jensen goes on to another. He produces two glass jars of sterilized water. Into one he dips his own well-washed hand, and sprinkles a few drops of the clean water into a sterilized petri dish. Into the other he dips a thoroughly dirty hand, and flicks a few drops onto the opposite end of the tray. Then he invites comparison of the two under the microscope.

Through these methods, he hopes to reach the dairymen who will be learning better techniques from his "extension" students. His ambition is to impress upon them all the direct connection between clean utensils, clean handling of milk and the health of their customers. The School of Agriculture students, he feels certain, will remember far better what they have glimpsed through the microscopes than any statistics he might quote to them on the growth of bacteria.

"Just let them see what happens," he says. "That's what they'll remember—not those astronomical numbers of bacteria to the inch."

Salvadoreans are receiving a different but no less practical course of instruction in sanitation in the home. New dwellings have been erected for the small land-holders of housing developments now mushrooming under government auspices. One of these, with 250 units, is twenty miles outside San Salvador, at Sitio del Niño, where a number of families are already settled. Trained home economists have been sent to teach the housewives how to handle facilities that have been strange to them, and the general care of their new brick homes.

These women had previously done their cooking over an open fire, often upon a flat rock inside their huts. Now they are asked to master the proper method of coping with kerosene stoves, to which they are being introduced for the first time. Each is taken through the whole proceeding until she understands it thoroughly, and is then required to prove her ability by filling and lighting the stove, before the instructor leaves her alone with it.

The home economist covers far more than the mysteries of the stove. She demonstrates the proper care of the wooden floors, how to handle garbage to discourage flies and how to get water from the nearby pump that has replaced the insanitary open wells. Most of the women plan to keep chickens and if possible a cow, and a few rules must also be laid down about the proper distance at which they should be kept from the house.

The men are taught the same techniques. If the parents have grasped the rudiments, the home-economics representatives are confident, the children will acquire them naturally.

In a country where extreme poverty has dominated the population for generations, and where the housing problem is so critical that some people live even now in the crater of an extinct volcano 2,500 feet down, it is not surprising that the occupants of brand-new brick homes must learn how to live in them.

But the learning is not all one-sided. The foreign technicians who have come to this territory to impart knowledge are also absorbing ideas that surprise them. Like others living for the first time as neighbors to active volcanoes (El Salvador has eleven), they are astonished to find highways covered with fine volcanic dust to the depth of two inches or more. They have marveled at the shrubbery and low trees along the roads, practically obscured by this dust, and have noted how pedestrians cover their heads and their faces with scarves to protect their noses and mouths against it as a vehicle passes.

Outsiders are continually surprised that, when mixed with the plowed soil, this dust has proved a stimulant rather than a detriment to vegetation. Once the particles have sifted over a field, Salvadoreans say, the young plants begin to shoot up at an accelerated rate, and flourish as they never did before.

The five men from New York headquarters of the United Nations carried back vivid memories of this strange dust, through which they drove for many a mile in broad daylight without ever glimpsing the sun, so thick was the "smog." They will remember especially a trip they took to Santa Catarina, of which Emil Corwin wrote:

"This town, some ninety-seven kilometers into the mountains, is outside the WHO Health Demonstration Area, but we visited it to see a BCG (tuberculosis vaccine) unit in operation. Dr. Rafael Vega-Gomez, in charge of the BCG field units, accompanied us on a wild ride during which we had a blowout, ran over a dog, lost our way, ran into a fog, and finally got stuck in volcanic silt while trying to make a steep grade. A passing farmer unhitched his oxen and used them to pull us out."

The prevalence of ox carts over motor vehicles, incidentally, was a paradox to the visitors, since they had found El Salvador so alert to the advantages of air transportation that it is deeply involved in co-operative efforts with other Central American countries to extend air transport service and to expand the facilities.

In this field El Salvador is working on a five-year program that will include establishment of a free airport, to service all of Central America and to accommodate both freight and passenger service to those countries. The meteorological and telecommunications facilities for the five countries co-operating will be co-ordinated for domestic flights, as will their security measures, and their laws and regulations for takeoffs and landings. This entire network will operate separately from the now routine international service. In all these plans, the ICAO is co-operating with Captain Horacio Melara, director of civil aviation for El Salvador.

Notwithstanding these developments, the population continues to maintain an ox cart philosophy, and about 30,000 of the vehicles are in operation. Because the country is small, surface transportation is not the complicated matter it has become in larger states, and the two-wheeled carts suit the majority of the people very well. Farmers prefer them to motor trucks because the cartage charge for ten kilometers is only about 1.6 cents for fifty pounds, or about $1.25 for a full cartload. Motor transport would cost many times that amount.

In addition to its regional co-operation on air transport, El Salvador has joined with its neighboring countries in a mutual effort to bring the locust plague under control. A joint agreement was signed in 1948, and headquarters were set up in Nicaragua, where the situation was most serious at that time. FAO was asked to act as a permanent technical adviser.

The value of this enterprise, in which participating states exchange information about breeding grounds, stage of development of the insects, direction of flights, types of locusts, weather conditions affecting their movements and the extent of damage to crops, was proved during an outbreak in Honduras in 1953. All the countries concerned took immediate action, which included dusting of the swarms by air as well as by hand in the fields. They checked the locusts at the point of origin, and prevented the spread of the menace to adjacent areas.

Thus the republic of El Salvador teeters between past and present, modern and medieval. Ox carts and airplanes. Reed huts and brick houses. Penicillin and "magic" charms. Such contrasts are commonplace in the life of the population.

The current administration realizes that no matter how intelligent and farsighted government planning may be, the pace of progress depends upon the people, and upon their understanding and co-operation. In this respect, President Osorio has not too much to complain about. But even he may be unaware of the extent of acceptance of the new ways that already exist among the residents of remote villages to which the New Yorkers penetrated in their rambles— Nejapa, for example, or Apopa, both of which have opened modern clinics with WHO advice and assistance.

In Nejapa, the staff operates in an old house that was once an antimalaria center—and still is, although it has shifted to contemporary methods. It is also a research laboratory, where sanitary engineers work on water problems, and public-health nurses handle the routine examinations. Members of the staff survey market conditions, with the aim of improving the cleanliness of the grounds, the containers for the various types of food sold, and the methods of preserving fish, vegetables and fruits. Not even the dogs that scamper about are immune to inspection.

The clinic nurses pay serious attention to the scores of superstitions current in the Nejapa area. Without attempting to counter these beliefs, they have listed many, realizing the importance of understanding customs and traditions that may influence a patient's reaction to treatment.

Among the jottings in this category the United Nations men read with interest: "if a bone gets stuck in your throat, turn a stick in the fire"; "a boy who looks at a drunken man will get diarrhea"; and "a pregnant woman risks losing her baby if she tells an unfriendly neighbor when the child is expected."

There was no need to point out the good-luck charms tied in little packets about the necks of the babies. Practically every infant was thus adorned. These small bags, the UN men were informed, contained beans, or maize—or a tooth. They are believed to ward off evil spirits.

Yet at Apopa the opposite side of the picture came into focus. A number of elderly men and women stood leisurely about the clinic there, as though awaiting instructions. Questions brought out that these were local civic leaders who had volunteered their support for the health center. More than that: they had formed a community society to get others stirred up about public health. Theirs is a dues-paying organization with a constitution and by-laws, and they hold frequent, formal meetings to decide on their self-appointed program and duties. Hospital boards in metropolitan centers, please note!

Once again, the people were in an enterprise up to the hilt. It is a safe wager that the general health situation in El Salvador will be showing marked advances within the next several years. The day may come when the fetishes will be tossed onto the rubbish heap, because in modern medicine the people will have found another, surer type of magic.

TWO

THE BACKGROUND AND FOREGROUND OF TECHNICAL ASSISTANCE

Six years after its wobbly beginnings in 1948, the Technical Assistance program of the United Nations has taken so firm a grip on the social consciousness of the world that it is doubtful whether even a global catastrophe could uproot the principles of international co-operation it has established. Paradoxically, nothing in its brief history has so enhanced its prospect of steady development as the financial crisis it underwent in 1953, from which it emerged with a few telltale scars, but more vigorous and more soundly entrenched than ever.

That period of stress, past but unforgotten, electrified parliaments and statesmen that had been laggard in their appropriations for the international fund. The moans that ascended from the deficient territories as projects were cut back drastically, as technicians were recalled and the props withdrawn from one promising venture after another, reverberated through legislative halls. Priorities long neglected were expedited, and checks for overdue payments went hastily into the mails.

Time and progress that were lost during those months of

struggle will be difficult to regain. Against that interval of gloom, however, can be balanced the probability that it will not be permitted to recur. Nations to whom "technical assistance" was only a puzzling phrase half a decade ago, can evaluate it accurately these days—and they do.

The basic concept, that stronger nations had a responsibility to help the less advanced lift themselves up to something approaching similar levels, crystallized slowly and rather timidly after the Second World War. Emergency rehabilitation and reconstruction work performed by UNRRA in that era probably set the pattern.

In his inaugural address on January 20, 1949, President Truman first outlined his Point Four program. His argument that investment of large sums in industrially retarded areas would speed progress, win friends for the democratic way of life and stimulate markets for exports caught the imagination of the world.

It brought a tremendous impetus to the movement already under way on a modest scale within the United Nations. In December of 1948, the General Assembly had set up its own program for economic development, and had included $288,000 in its regular budget appropriations for activities of this unit during 1949. They were to cover mainly social-welfare projects and aid for governments in problems of administration, through the assignment of qualified advisers in those fields.

Today, these operations continue as before, as a part of the United Nations regular activities, and are known as the Technical Assistance Administration.

In June of 1949 delegates assembled as usual at Geneva

for the summer session of the Economic and Social Council of the United Nations, which controls the TA. To it came the United States representatives, aglow with enthusiasm for the potentialities of the Point Four program, then in the process of organization. They laid before the council a proposal that the nations adopt these objectives on a world scale, to accelerate the advancement of less favored populations everywhere. Each government would pledge according to its means, not only cash but also its technical talent, to help its needy neighbors help themselves. Latin American republics strongly seconded the plan.

There and then the "expanded program of technical assistance" of the United Nations was born. Based on the belief that if given a gentle shove in the right direction, many backward populations would generate their own steam and build their own prosperity, it came into being as a pool of resources and skills, to be used for the benefit of all. Time has more than justified this idealism.

Cash had first to be raised, and methods of operation worked out. Pledges were invited, and fifty-five participating nations subscribed $20,070,260, of which $17,354,013 was produced on the barrel head during the first eighteen months.

The field work would be handled by staff members of agencies, even then busy at their specialized tasks in many corners of the world, all of whom were affiliates of the United Nations.

Up to this point they had been financed separately, from governmental sources, and without monetary support from the United Nations. They continue as before to administer their own regular budgets, now supplemented by allocations from ETAP, the Expanded Technical Assistance Program. Within this framework, the TAA constitutes one of several participating agencies.

These are: the Food and Agriculture Organization (FAO); International Labor Organization (ILO); World Health Organization (WHO); United Nations Educational, Scientific and Cultural Organization (UNESCO); International Civil Aviation Organization (ICAO); International Telecommunication Union (ITU), and World Meteorological Organization (WMO).

Executives of these organizations function as a co-ordinating group for all, known as the Technical Assistance Board. David Owen of Canada is the executive director.

To the list must be added the United Nations Children's Fund (UNICEF), which is not a specialized agency. Its close teamwork with the WHO brings its representatives intimately into the field operations of that group, however, to an extent that defies segregation.

Paralleling the efforts of all these units are the International Bank for Reconstruction and Development (called simply "the Bank"), which advances loans to individual governments for economic or social-development schemes; and the International Monetary Fund, which helps to stabilize currencies in the areas of so-called soft money.

Outside the United Nations and separate from it, are also the Point Four of the United States, under its present title of Foreign Operations Administration; and the British Colombo Plan, organized to stimulate progress especially in southeastern Asia.

Rivalries among the groups in the early stages were inevitable. Supervision over projects and territories came into dispute. Increasing co-ordination among them has minimized duplication of effort. Their current fusion and harmony, however, can be attributed to one implacable, admitted fact. Contrasted with the mountain of human deprivation they are called upon to tackle, their massed strength and their merged resources are so puny that they shrink to molehill proportions. In the face of this grim reality, overlapping has become unthinkable.

As the expanded program of Technical Assistance got under way, its administrators found themselves groping cautiously along unexplored paths. They were clear about what they proposed to do, but baffled by dozens of unforeseen complications for which they had to work out their own formulas.

A major poser was the reluctance of governments of the underdeveloped areas to accept the assistance offered. Actually, despite the outcries by its detractors that technical assistance is a prodigious "give-away" of vast sums, it has never had that character. Firm conditions have always been imposed that potential recipients of this type of aid produce what are known as "matching funds," as well as equipment, and personnel to be trained to take over the completed project. Only then would contracts be considered, and foreign advisers sent.

Jealous guardians of the sovereignty of newly independent nations greeted these policies with utmost suspicion. Open their borders to foreigners who might infiltrate their lands and hoax them out of their natural resources? This was risky.

Isolate funds for long-term programs, when cash was so short and scarcities so great? This was difficult. So instead of rushing into the arms of the United Nations with whoops of welcome, officials of the needy countries squared away challengingly, demanding guarantees of sincerity and good faith. After repeated, earnest explanations, they inched their way into the program like timid bathers inserting their toes into chilly waters, before deciding to take the plunge.

All projects submitted, they discovered, had to be weighed for their ultimate value to the population as a whole—not to the government temporarily in power. Many were rejected as impractical, badly planned or too ambitious. Revisions were demanded. A few passed the test, and implementation began.

The initial screenings of the applications took so long that funds available continued largely intact. Impatience was voiced. Protests began to come in from the donor governments that large reserves were still in hand, and that the second pledging session was impending. Why should they be called upon for further contributions, they demanded, when so much remained unspent?

At the close of the first fiscal period, covering eighteen months, 1952 pledges were called for, and only $18,795,355 was listed. Yet requests had begun to accelerate as the poorer countries and territories gained appreciation of the opportunities offered. Before 1953 dawned, the tempo of contracts signed between ETAP and the governments clamoring for its aid was bringing the program into rough financial weather.

Springtime of 1953 found the situation crucial. The parliaments of donor countries had dallied so long in appropriating funds to meet their pledges that cash due on contracts already made was neither in the treasury nor in prospect. Severe measures were called for if ETAP was to remain financially sound. They were taken regretfully, in the form of sharp cutbacks in plans approved earlier, and in postponement of excellent projects that were acutely necessary in specific areas. Each slash in the program brought groans of disappointment from local authorities, who could reckon the cost of the delays in terms of epidemics unchecked in their districts, or loss of crops through the spread of parasites, or rising unemployment.

The crisis had one fortunate result—the drastic steps that had to be taken shook the world into belated realization of the role ETAP had assumed on the international scene. Legislative bodies waked to the conviction that they must vote their appropriations more promptly or be prepared to share responsibility for delayed benefits to other lands. The Technical Assistance Board looked squarely at its dilemma of hand-to-mouth existence and announced:

"This won't do. What is needed here for the most effective results is planning on a five-year basis. But at least, we must hold pledging conferences earlier, and know before any given year opens what we will have to spend."

This much has been gained. The 1954 pledging conference was held at headquarters in New York, in November of 1953. Attendance set a record, and subscriptions reached a new peak. Of the total of $24,000,000 promised, the TAB has cannily earmarked $3,000,000 to be left unexpended, as a reserve. A like amount will be added annually until $12,-

000,000 has accumulated, as a cushion against possible further lapses in payments, and insurance that commitments can be met.

Taxpayers around the world are footing the bill. Miniscule as each individual contribution has been, it has counted. This generation, that has learned to live with the realities of atomic power and the potentialities of the hydrogen bomb, counts itself cynical. It is still the same generation about which the English historian, Arnold J. Toynbee, has written that it may be best remembered because it brought "the first age since the dawn of history in which mankind dared to believe it practicable to make the benefits of civilization available to the whole human race."

As to where their money goes, the specialized agencies are eager to demonstrate to the taxpayers, within the limits of practicality. One of the best methods they have found to date is a vicarious globe-trotting expedition via a motion-picture camera equipped with sound tape. No medium is better equipped to recreate the sights, sounds, colors or character of distant communities and populations. It also telescopes time, and within an interval of minutes can present before-and-after stages in a community, between which months may have elapsed. Documentaries of this sort have been made by the dozens, and more are being added year by year.

Snugly reeled on their spools and labeled as to subject matter, films made by capable camera crews in color and in black and white are accumulating in a special library in the Secretariat building. They run from five minutes to a full hour in length, averaging ten to fifteen minutes, and are obtainable at extremely nominal rentals, with narration in any of several languages. Schools, libraries, universities and clubs use the rental service regularly, yet their total audience remains meager in comparison with those millions who are still unaware that they exist.

Routines for the diversified programs they depict are well established now, and the machinery of administration and supply meshes fairly smoothly. An imaginary project will illustrate.

Somewhere in the Pacific lies an island whose people rely mainly upon fishing for their livelihood. They have no schools, only limited crops of grain, not very skillfully cultivated, and practically no medical services except for native healers. Gradually, their fishing grounds are becoming depleted. Their catches are fewer and smaller, and hunger threatens their families since they depend upon sails and oars and the sphere of their operations is limited. Their government calls upon ETAP for help—for an expert who can explain what has driven the fish away, and how they may be lured back.

The officials add that they would like other kinds of help as well. Their fruit trees are withering from a blight they do not understand; they have a good deal of unemployment. Their island is too small to boast an airport, and too far off the trade lanes to support any but local commerce.

A survey of the situation is always the first move. Pinpointing the island on a map, ETAP representatives in New York estimate that time and expense can be saved by dispatching specialists from New Zealand to make a report. Names of two possible candidates are plucked from a unique world file of qualified authorities, built up during the last six years. Explanatory cables are sent, asking both men to visit the island and advise what is needed.

Back comes word that neither is available. One is hospitalized, recovering from an operation; the other is away on a journey of months. The map is consulted once more, and routes charted. What about the Philippines? There's an eminent specialist in Manila who would be invaluable on the fruit-tree blight. He is farther away, but could fly part of the way. And there are two Australians, either of whom is equipped to analyze fishing-industry problems. Presently the posts have been filled and the surveyors are en route to the trouble spot.

Arrived at their destination, these experienced men take first things first. Before plunging into the business at hand, they set about establishing cordial relations with the natives. Even if it means delay, this is an essential.

In regions like this, the sun is the clock. Life has its own pace, and the people cannot be hurried without risking confusion and resentment. Each stage in the survey must be explained and discussed with the island officials, so that they will understand and will continue to co-operate. Their own opinions are sought, tactfully and often with illuminating results, since all localities have their peculiarities and local leaders usually are best informed about them.

Six weeks later the reports are ready and the recommendations of the experts are at hand. The Australian has solved the mystery of the disappearing fish. They are still in the area, but have moved out beyond the range of the islanders' craft, to a rich new feeding ground created for them by relatively minor volcanic disturbances in the ocean bed. The Manila specialist has identified the cause of the fruit blight, and has advised both spraying with the proper chemicals and replanting of the trees at wider intervals. He has suggested that the soil is capable of sustaining other types of fruits, and that better seed and more careful cultivation would surely increase the grain yields.

Out of experience in his own country, the Filipino has noted that many of the islanders are suffering from yaws and malaria, and that malnutrition is extensive. He has talked with the island leaders about the WHO program, and has proposed that they ask for medical help, in addition to equipment and supplies to meet their other needs.

The next stage is a contract signed between ETAP and the island executives. It commits ETAP to send a mission that will include medical, agricultural and fishing industry experts for one year's stay, to carry out definite projects for which the island administration undertakes to raise the equivalent of $50,000—a large sum for such a community. ETAP is committed to pay the travel expenses and salaries of these men, and to furnish a part of the necessary paraphernalia and supplies.

Under the supervision of the TA representative in the region, the entire program enters its active phase with the arrival of the mission members. Fortunately both the Filipino and the Australian technicians who made the survey are included, and are welcomed back by the islanders as old friends.

Piled up on the dock where it had been unloaded by a cargo steamer, the mission men find a consignment of part of their supplies. They check over the quantities of hand tools they had ordered, as best suited to these unskilled farmers; bundles of seedling fruit trees with which they will experiment; bags of grain seed of superior quality, hitherto unknown in this island; and hand sprayers with which to attack both the parasite that has claimed the fruit crop and the malaria that menaces health. The Children's Fund has sent quantities of DDT, penicillin and drums of powdered milk.

With a year in which to effect the changes planned, the technicians get to work in earnest. Instruction for the population in the newer methods and the unfamiliar tools is imperative. Otherwise the relapse will be rapid, once this team has taken ship for home. 888407

The Australian burrows into the freight the steamer has delivered and comes up with an outboard motor. Its appearance is the signal for general excitement. Native fishermen surge around him, jibbering with anticipation. They have seen the speedy P-T boats used by the Navy during the war, and know how much farther and faster mechanized craft can range then their own sailboats. Wherever the fish have gone, they will soon be on their trail. In no time, one of their own light boats has been dragged farther up on the beach, and the motor attached. Then—comes disillusionment. Hardly has the scull been launched than it sinks in a few feet of water.

Thunderstruck, they gape at their Australian friend. He is working busily, directing the lifting of the boat, but he does not seem too much disturbed. Actually, knowing what would happen he has chosen to let them discover for themselves by demonstration, that there will be risks involved in improper handling of their new treasure.

Presently he gathers them around him on the beach and discusses their mutual problem. This is a fairly powerful motor—too heavy for their light boats. More motors will be coming, therefore they must construct sturdier craft, to sustain them. The fish will be safe for a while longer—as long as it takes to build at least one of the newer models. For the longer expeditions ahead, they had better be a bit larger over-all. They nod comprehendingly, inspecting the sketches he pulls from his pocket.

The boatbuilding activities turn naturally into an open-air school room, with the Australian as teacher. Long after he is gone, many craft will be built intelligently by these natives, with understanding of the requirements. But the day the first of the series is completed and triumphantly launched, he is as proud as any of the islanders. It is beautifully seaworthy.

Off they set at last. The Australian expert bends over a mystifying apparatus these fishermen have never seen, and sets their course according to strange little characters traced on a revolving drum. To them it is magic. To him, it is a sonar finder—an adaptation of equipment originally used in wartime to hunt submarines, and now improved to the point at which it transmits and records the movement of large schools of fish. He assures them that he will teach some of their younger men to operate it later.

Presently they are farther out than they have ever gone before, and the Australian is signaling—this is the place. The motor is cut off and down go the nets. In no time they are struggling to lift them back—heavy with fish bigger and plumper than they have seen in many months. They have found the happy hunting grounds that the fish had discovered so much sooner, through their own finny telegraph system!

As the weeks roll by, the natives learn many things. Some become mechanics, expert in repairing the motors for the fishing fleet. Others have qualified to keep in condition the new hoes, rakes and weeders that are becoming familiar to the farmers. Still others have grown adept at spraying the fruit trees, from which the blight is disappearing, or at coaxing the new seedlings into healthy growth.

The island has had clinic after clinic. Penicillin has been administered to many, and yaws has relaxed its crippling hold on former victims. Malaria, "the shaking disease," has been reduced by the DDT sprayings and the draining of a large swamp where its mosquito carriers thrived. The new grain has been planted in properly fertilized earth, and is flourishing. Life is busier and more satisfying than ever it was before. The year of the contract is still young, and now that the population is better fed and more hopeful, the mission team has begun a mild type of agitation.

"You have no schools here," they comment. "Why don't you learn to read and write, so that your children and you will be able to understand all these printed directions we have been giving you? After we leave, who is going to read them for you?"

The native leaders consider the matter thoughtfully. Parents nod in agreement. Some day the island will have its own school, its own teachers. The next generation must know better how to handle its affairs. When the possibility of United Nations fellowships is explained, the leaders beam delightedly. And eventually the cargo steamer takes aboard two young islanders, daringly headed for Australia and an education.

This is the way ETAP prepares the populations of backward areas to help themselves. Some benefits from its projects are speedy and visible. Most of them take hold only gradually, and there are discouraging backslidings. Nature and tradition must be taken into account. Floods and earthquakes can upset timetables, and local political quarrels can wreck the best of programs. All of these have happened, and will continue to happen. Even if the entire TA program were obliterated at one swoop, however, the hopes it has roused and the mentalities it has awakened would carry the spiral on under its own power for a long time to come.

Populations once disheartened have felt the stirrings of national pride and self-confidence. They know now that they can give as well as receive, and will not easily relinquish their unaccustomed capacity of teacher as well as student of better ways of life for all. For ETAP has conceded that the smallest of nations have treasuries of skills and of mentalities as valuable as those the great powers can provide, in quality if not in quantity. They glory in this recognition.

Take the case of Saint Lucia, in the British Windward Islands. Its government wrote to ask ETAP whether it could cite any countries which had experience in harnessing underground geysers, to provide electric power. ETAP wrote back to say that it knew of two—Italy and Iceland. Back came a request from the Saint Lucians, to have an Icelandic engineer sent to survey their potentialities in this field. The

Icelander was assigned, made his survey, and submitted his report.

The project was feasible. He had estimated the costs and the time that would be required. Soon a contract had been drawn, examined and approved. Saint Lucia would put up the sum stipulated, and asked that the same Icelander direct the work. He was commissioned, the underground geysers were successfully capped, and they are now driving motors, speeding up industry and lighting homes in Saint Lucia.

Pridefully, then, little Iceland takes rank with the great nations, among the sponsors of Technical Assistance. She herself is a recipient of aid from the program, but in a mutual exchange among friends, who can lose face?

In ETAP, no one nation can claim any monopoly. At Geneva in the autumn of 1953, the USSR announced unexpectedly that it was prepared to join the pool—but on certain conditions. The Soviet government offered an initial gift of rubles equivalent to $1,000,000, but stipulated that its contribution was not to be administered by any of the specialized agencies, since it then held membership in none of them. This conflict with the regulations made the donation unacceptable, and Moscow was so advised.

The matter was threshed out over the ensuing months, during which the director general of the TAA, Hugh Keenleyside of Canada, visited the Soviet Union to point out that the basis on which the program operates is universally applicable, and unalterable. In a message to Secretary General Dag Hammarskjold, the Soviet government eventually made the concessions necessary, and its check was belatedly accepted.

During the spring of 1954, the USSR further surprised United Nations circles by affiliating with the ILO and UNESCO—two of the specialized agencies it had boycotted and denounced for years. Some of the Soviet bloc nations quickly followed this lead and announced their acceptance of provisions of the agency charters, which, for member countries of the UN, is tantamount to automatic member-- ship. Exactly how, and to what extent, the death of Stalin has affected Kremlin policies in this as in other respects, remains a topic for conjecture.

Because statistics in quantities are merely boring, they have been kept to a minimum in these pages. Fundamentally, it is personalities that count. Upon them ETAP will founder or flourish—upon the men and women who are grappling at close quarters with the ills of the world, and upon the character and the capacities of the populations who are daily bringing to them their manifold problems, and waiting trustfully to be shown the solutions.

In both these groups the free world has a keenly important stake. The fieldworkers are its deputies, and its envoys. They have been sent to heal the sick, to banish famine if possible and to build better habitations for those miserably sheltered. Unless they also build friendship and understanding, the repercussions will sow fertile soil for Communist and other agitators. There have been failures, but they have been minor ones.

Our stake in the native peoples is equally vital. Every fractional rise in their living standards brings them farther out of their isolation, closer to us and toward greater security for all. As they edge their way into the ebb and flow of world trade, they emerge more distinctly as the market of the future—relatively untapped and almost limitless in scope. Decades will elapse before these rehabilitated territories will begin to be saturated with all those commodities and facilities that have brought this era unprecedented comfort and more blessings than man ever knew before.

Time has been short, and the total investment ridiculously low in comparison with the billions that are being poured into all manner of weapons for defense and offense—just in case. The momentum is stepping up, however. It is apparent now that the contributing nations are backing, in ETAP, one of the most promising stocks yet offered on any exchange.

It has been bought "at bottom." Barring a world cataclysm, it has no place to go but up.

THREE

LAND OF POTENTIAL PLENTY

ETHIOPIA

THUNDER MUTTERED on the horizon, that morning early in 1953. The air was still, and heavy with the threat of rain. In a field beside a road that leads out from Addis Ababa, three natives and a white man in Western dress crouched above a patch of small green sprouts of flax, ignoring the gathering storm clouds. Michael W. Millar, Canadian expert on seeds with the FAO mission in Ethiopia, was checking on one of his experiments.

Up the asphalt road from the capital came bowling a little motorcade. In the lead was a big black Cadillac. Four or five older, smaller cars snuffed along behind like hounds on the scent. On a stretch of pavement only a hundred yards beyond the absorbed group in the field, the procession halted. His attention caught, Millar looked up and, without rising, swung about to eye this diversion.

"That would be the emperor," he said to himself.

He was right. As he watched, a uniformed guard leaped from one of the vehicles to open the door of the black sedan. Haile Selassie, small in stature but great in dignity, stepped out unhurriedly. He paused for a moment, a slight figure in a white suit, the familiar sun helmet topping his face with its full dark beard. Then with great deliberation he paced up and down, studying the piles of crushed rock and the strewn timbers that testified to repair work in progress.

There was not much to see, and the average passer-by would have spared it hardly a conscious glance. The emperor, on the contrary, seemed to find it absorbing. He lingered, solitary and thoughtful, checking on the completed patches and the general condition of the thoroughfare—originally built by the Italians when they occupied his country and he lived abroad in exile. At length he re-entered his sedan, the guards hopped back to their places, and the ruler and his retinue disappeared over the next rise.

"That was typical," Mr. Millar said about the emperor recently, while in New York on his way back to Canada after fourteen months in Ethiopia. "Haile Selassie is every inch a leader and the greatest man in his realm, bar none.

"He is making heroic efforts to stimulate progress for his people in every sphere, but he is thwarted by a lack of trained subordinates to carry out the programs he is constantly planning. If his ministers were as far-visioned as Haile Selassie himself, the momentum of advancement in that country would be phenomenal," the Canadian added, "but he must depend upon the staff he has, and they are not yet equipped to appreciate or co-ordinate the projects the emperor sets in motion. Everything lags until orders come down from the palace. Then things really hum. That's why Selassie himself tries to be everywhere and to see everything.

"The roads—for instance. I've seen that big black car of his frequently, rolling up the highway and then standing while the emperor goes over every inch of the ground at a given point. He knows better than anyone how essential those roads are to Ethiopia, where transport is the most expensive in the world, I'm sure. He has a $5,000,000 loan from the International Bank to build new roads and to repair the ones the Italians left behind them. That amount wouldn't buy more than a good-sized spur in many countries, but with the force of laborers he has at hand and the native stone, Haile Selassie is stretching it out to create a really healthy network. Bedded with crushed rock and surfaced with tar, the result is a pretty fair road—absolutely imperative for bringing produce up out of the interior, to the coast. That's why the emperor makes all those expeditions—to see how the work is coming along."

Exports are important to most countries but to Ethiopia they are vital, Mr. Millar explained. They bring into the country a flow of urgently needed capital with which to exploit its almost untapped resources, and to elevate its population gradually from its present backward status to one of normal living standards and educational opportunities.

Nature has been almost overwhelmingly generous to these people, with its bounty of fertile soil and teeming vegetation, capable of supplying food far beyond their national needs. To sell these surpluses for the foreign exchange that will purchase modern machinery, vehicles, public utilities and medical services now lacking, roads are imperative, to transport their goods from the hinterland to the ports.

"Situated almost exactly in the heart of Africa, Ethiopia may one day pump forth a bloodstream of great agricultural riches not only to its neighbors but also to the world beyond," begins the section on Ethiopia in the fifth report of the Technical Assistance Board of the United Nations, issued in the spring of 1953. Mr. Millar heartily concurred.

"Men who know farming in other countries stand agog when they get to Ethiopia and survey the wealth inherent in agriculture there," he said. "Millions upon millions of bushels of wheat and barley are ready and waiting for shipment overseas. The country could easily become the granary of the entire Middle East, these crops flourish so bountifully. Coffee—of superb quality—grows wild. There are plenty of coffee plantations, and they have coffee forests as well. The natives simply chop down the shrubs, when they get too thick around their homes.

"They can grow cotton extensively in the warmer parts of Ethiopia, yet so little has been done about it that they are spending $20,000,000 annually to import cotton from other nations. The Irish flax we introduced there—the Stormount Gossamer variety—sprang up and grew better, even, than it does in Ireland. It reached a meter in height. And as for cattle, in which the Ethiopians reckon their wealth, they must have at least 19,000,000 head."

All that Mr. Millar had to say about the potentialities of Ethiopian agriculture has been said before him by other experts of the United Nations and of the United States Point Four program, who are or have been in the country advising the government on different projects. Their work goes slowly because it must be accommodated to the tempo of an unschooled population. In many of its phases, it will be a number of years before the pace accelerates noticeably. There is, however, evidence now of marked improvement in others—for example, in the campaign to eliminate rinderpest from the cattle herds. This was begun with UNRRA funds, and has been carried on since 1948 by veterinarians sent in by the FAO. The ailment is usually fatal. Its symptoms are a discharge from the eyes of the suffering animal, and consistent loss of weight until death occurs. Until science produced an antidote, millions of head were lost through it annually. Beef so infected is dangerous for humans, and the export market is automatically closed to any country where it is even suspected, until rigid inspection confirms that it has disappeared.

As that initial FAO mission moved out into the countryside, its members met stout resistance from the Ethiopian farmers, who never had heard of vaccinations for cattle and were panicked at what they regarded as the murderous designs of the foreigners.

In some areas violence flared, and the project had to be suspended until an educational campaign could be carried out with the full backing of the government. The FAO men spent their time traveling from place to place with native interpreters, discussing the disease that had been commonplace in the country for ages past, answering questions and reiterating the advantages the treatments would bring. Gradually the excitement and uproar subsided, and the owners were coaxed to permit vaccination of some of their cattle.

Statistics from Ethiopia now offer no hint of the obstacles that have been faced and surmounted, nor of the diplomacy the FAO men had to exercise throughout those beginning stages. Photographs made then, however, reflect the dramatic scenes that took place as the tribes assembled in a semi-circle, usually against a background of their mud-and-straw huts, to confront these aliens who wanted to plunge needles into their valuable cows.

Bareheaded, clad invariably in white cotton suits with their capelike *shammas* (coats) slung over one shoulder, the Ethiopians stood silent and suspicious, each clasping in one hand a six-foot wooden staff, while interpreters explained about the vaccine and the benefits it would bring to their cherished herds. Time after time in these tableaux, tension was eased and the farmers' anger mollified through the quiet announcement that their emperor knew about—and ap-proved—these strange proceedings that were being recom-mended to them.

Eventually it became easier to induce the owners to queue up to pay the small fee originally levied for the vaccinations. A small table would be set in the open before one of the huts, and a tribal leader would sit there, checking the lists. Then the whole assembly would move to the corrals, where com-petent, white-smocked natives, already coached in their duties, assisted as the animals were led up and the long needles thrust into their necks by the FAO men, in ranchers' outfits of checkered shirts, beige trousers and Stetsons.

Those first patient, cautious demonstrations have paid off handsomely. As the vaccinations took hold and herds in one area after another picked up health and strength, the word was passed from tribe to tribe.

Suspicion has long since vanished, in favor of confidence and hospitality for the veterinarians. Haile Selassie gave the drive an added impetus by ordering cancellation of the vaccination fees, in order to spread the operations as rapidly as possible to the maximum number of cattle. Thereafter, opposition dwindled even faster.

Several circumstances differentiated the vaccination drive in Ethiopia from a similar one in Afghanistan. More cattle were involved, the owners and the herds were less nomadic and consequently more accessible, and a slightly more regular schedule could be followed. Imported supplies were used at first, but the emperor favored domestic production as soon as it could be arranged.

Two years were needed to set up a production plant in Addis Ababa for the vaccine, and especially to procure the freezing and drying equipment that were indispensable to keep the virus sufficiently potent. Formerly cultured only in tissue at a cost of about $1.00 per shot, it is now obtainable through the use of eggs, chickens, goats or pigs, for approximately three cents, and gives lifetime immunity against rinderpest. The earlier types had been effective only temporarily.

In 1949, the FAO team managed to vaccinate only 20,000 animals. By 1951 the total had risen to 361,740, and in 1952 it reached 587,000. In the early part of 1953, when domestic buyers of meat had begun refusing to purchase any animal that had not been vaccinated, 4,000 head per month were being marketed at Asmara, and the veterinarians' cause was won.

Until the arrival of FAO in the country, nearly five years ago, Ethiopian beef was taboo for export because of the prevalence of rinderpest, and the danger it harbors for humans as well as animals. But the humpbacked Ethiopian cows represent a tremendous source of good beef when their health can be attested by sanitary inspectors. The day is now not far off when sides or quarters can be shipped with perfect safety to foreign consumers.

Meat-hungry nations have been eying this progress against the disease in Ethiopia with keen interest, because they know that it promises a vast source of supply. The Israeli government in particular has been forehanded in conducting negotiations with the administrators of Haile Selassie. It has already established a freezing plant in Ethiopia, near the coast, from which it will be possible to ship beef. Other such installations are in prospect.

In addition to beef cattle, the Ethiopians have great numbers of pigs to offer, especially because they themselves do not eat pork, due to religious prejudices.

However, until and unless the gap in the road network from the interior to the coast can be spanned, export of cattle from Ethiopia in volume will remain more of a prospect than a reality. At present the major channel of transport to Djibouti, the port in French Somaliland, is the single railroad, owned by the French. Freight costs, added to the ocean freight, are so high that the herd owners are unable to sell their animals at existing prices, and the prospective buyer nations cannot pay enough to cover these costs. This problem remains to be solved. There is a motor road that leads north from Addis Ababa to the port of Assab in Eritrea. But the cattle from the southeast, south and southwest parts of the country must still somehow be brought to the capital area before they can be loaded on trucks for this trip, and a large enough fleet of trucks must be available for the haulage to Assab. This alternative, therefore, hardly represents a solution.

Identical transport difficulties confront the Ethiopian administrators in their efforts to increase their exports of coffee, which currently account for about fifty per cent of the country's foreign income. With the abundance and the quality of the coffee beans, there is little doubt that this precentage could be rapidly and materially increased if the transport difficulties could be removed and the shipping costs reduced.

Alert to the undeveloped possibilities of the coffee crop, the Ethiopian government asked for help on it from the FAO. From Haiti, which has for a long time produced excellent coffee, the FAO summoned Dr. Pierre Sylvain. With one interval of home leave, Dr. Sylvain has been in Ethiopia since 1951, checking on the available types of coffee, suggesting improved methods of selection so that plantations might concentrate on the most profitable varieties, and advising about routines of preparation in order to lift the prestige of the Ethiopian brands on the world market.

Under his guidance several innovations have been adopted for the grading and labeling of beans before packing, and groups of Ethiopians are being trained as tasters and sorters. New designs in packaging and identification have been planned to rescue the product from its handicaps of past years, when as Michael Millar expressed it, "the world's best coffee came onto the market as just about the world's worst." Once the basic transport problem has been worked out, the coffee exporters should be ready with modern packing and labeling facilities that will command recognition and respect from nations where the consumption of the brew is steadily mounting.

Meanwhile Dr. Sylvain has identified and collected in Ethiopia fourteen new varieties of coffee, which are now being cultivated and tested in Brazil, Colombia and Costa Rica. Even while Ethiopia remains a recipient country in the United Nations Technical Assistance program, therefore, she is already contributing to the economic development of other nations.

The domestic market for coffee in Ethiopia is negligible. Under their religious strictures, Ethiopians abstain from both tobacco and alcohol, as well as pork, and although they drink some coffee, they consume greater quantities of other liquids.

"A cup of coffee" plays no part in the daily life, but local social observances have a definite warmth and charm. In the rural areas, as distinct from the towns, the people are hospitable in the extreme, and it is usual for any farmer to offer a guest a glass of *talla* (a kind of beer made from barley), or the more acceptable *tej*, concocted of fermented honey. The visitor is also apt to be invited to remain overnight.

If he accepts, he will sleep upon straw laid upon eucalyptus laths, on a cotlike bed about twelve inches off the floor. He will share the family meal, served on the ground outside the hut and consisting of the native bread, eaten with stew.

The bread made from the pulverized seeds of a plant called *teff*—which resembles timothy—is a circular pancake about a foot in diameter. It is baked over an open fire on a tin tray of the same size and shape. Fragments are pinched off and used as a scoop for the stew, known as *wat*, which is hot with onions and peppers.

Most of these farm families are illiterate and very poor, yet their friendliness and openheartedness are delightful and their courtesy almost extravagant. They work hard and with little help from modern equipment or modern ideas, except those brought to them by the visiting technicians. A large share of the labor falls to the women, even in the fields, until it comes to plowing. This is exclusively the man's task. If a farmer owns oxen, he uses them hitched to a primitive plow with a wooden blade to break the earth. For reaping, the natives here, as in Afghanistan, were accustomed to a hand sickle. When scythes were brought in and demonstrated the men stood about full of curiosity and wonder, and immediately showed a desire to try out the new tool, although they proved inept at keeping the blades sharp, or at repairing a broken part. They will need consistent instruction before the scythe becomes firmly established in Ethiopian agriculture.

On the other hand, a single, progressive farmer can exercise a potent influence on an entire area. Following a tip from the Ministry of Agriculture, Mr. Millar wangled a truck and went bumping and jolting over the countryside to Sire, in the province of Arussi, to make the acquaintance of Ato Birru. It was a two-day trip, and well worth the effort.

Ato (a minor title) Birru is a little scrap of a man, seventy years old and weighing about 100 pounds. He is a real "son of the soil," with that instinctive understanding of the earth and its bounty that defies borders or birth. For good measure, he is also an excellent businessman—and a humanitarian. His compound is run according to his own ideas, which frequently do not jibe with those of his compatriots.

When his unannounced guest arrived, Ato Birru had to be summoned from the field where he was busy with his twenty-five workmen, pulling up weeds. He was pleased to show the FAO man around, and to the visitor the next several hours proved to be an interlude of unadulterated delight.

As a specialist on seeds, Mr. Millar was gratified to find that the old man was growing experimentally every type of seed the FAO had introduced into the country. Ato Birru even had at hand a crop that Millar had personally sponsored—the Irish flax—which they inspected together and discussed from the point of view of its diverse uses.

Ethiopians have grown oil flax for a thousand years, but the tests with linen flax date back only to 1950. For the present it is under consideration mainly as a future source for heavy twine and binders for the domestic market as well as for export, since the people have no experience in weaving it for cloth, as the Irish do. Commercial interests are watching these developments closely, though, for they believe the production of cloth is bound to come. Some co-operatives have already been formed for its exploitation at the proper time.

Ato Birru was well aware of the possibilities of his flax crop, Millar found, and had progressed in his plans even beyond the relatively rapid growth of the twine-and-binder stage. His workmen were paid in cash, rather than on the usual scale of one third of the crop—or fifty per cent on irrigated land. They received straight salaries of $15

(Ethiopian) per month, which represented a definite departure from the time-honored, feudal system. Ato Birru also provided each man with a *turkel*, or mud hut, for his family, and two suits of clothing per year, consisting of white cotton shirts and shorts. To make the clothes, he maintained a tailor the year around, on his property.

Ato Birru reported that his flax harvest would be expanded gradually to meet commercial demands, but he was calculating also how much he might need to insure that the clothing his men receive would eventually be made from homegrown flax. His holdings were located in an area too cool for cotton fields, therefore he had been compelled to purchase the material he had used to date. If his reckonings evolve as the old man expected, he will soon be well ahead of his farmer friends in his linen-weaving project.

The FAO man saw no reason to be skeptical on this point. Every phase of Ato Birru's farm offered proof of his competence and vision. Mr. Millar was shown one vast field of about 100 acres planted with white beans—for export—in which the rows stood as geometrically perfect as though set by machine. Yet the job had been done largely by hand. Ten teams of oxen and thirty workmen had handled it.

Quietly and without self-consciousness, the old farmer pointed out that his highly individual methods had made his land a profitable investment even by Western standards. A touch of pride crept into his voice, however, as he assured the Canadian that he was disinterested in purchasing luxuries for himself which he could well afford, such as an automobile or a stately home. When the guest asked to be shown his host's residence, Ato Birru pointed out precisely the same kind of mud hut as those in which his employees lived. The furnishings were identical as well—a few simple stools and a straw-covered bed, and the same tin plates, knives and forks as the laborers owned.

Ato Birru was childless, but he had acquired a large foster family by adoption from among his neighbors. Each youngster he took under his wing was insured as much education as the district had to offer. Some of the more intelligent had been sent abroad, with the help of the Ethiopian government, for study and training. In years to come, one or more of these hopefuls may carry forward in Arussi province the leadership that their courageous and forward-looking benefactor has firmly established.

In his sponsorship of these students Ato Birru's attitude closely parallels that of the emperor, who holds the portfolio of minister of education in his own cabinet, out of conviction that the school system is of the first importance to his nation. Haile Selassie, though handicapped by lack of funds, has been unremitting in his efforts to provide more schools and to improve the educational system generally. It is an indication of his readiness to adopt modern methods that the largest group of foreigners now active in Ethiopia—about 300 in all—are employed in his ministry.

Mr. Millar found young Ethiopians surprisingly quick to learn, and "with minds like sponges." They retained what they had absorbed, too, but he commented frankly that an uncomfortably large number of these students appear to have little desire to translate their knowledge into action.

"There's a gap," he said. "The background of a feudal society that has existed for hundreds of years tends to convince these young Ethiopians that they have become aristocrats of a sort, merely because they have been educated. Most of them seek out some white-collar job in which they can let their fingernails grow and grow (I've seen some at least two inches long and very daintily exhibited), instead of realizing the value and satisfaction of some kind of mechanical or agricultural labor that would give good returns to themselves and to their country. Only a few seem to realize that physical work is not degrading, and that the others are being a bit pompous. Things will improve gradually, I guess, as the number of literate people in Ethiopia gets larger, and ceases to be an elite group."

Meanwhile Haile Selassie himself continues to demonstrate his appreciation of the hard work of trained men. However, few of the foreign technicians acting as advisers in his country have ever had access to him, although they are frequently conscious of his interest in their projects, and of his efforts to keep in touch with developments.

It came as quite a surprise, therefore, when E. H. F. Swain, an Australian specialist in forestry who had been on the job for two years, was summoned for an audience one day.

When he was conducted in to meet the emperor, Mr. Swain was astonished to find himself involved in a very detailed discussion of what he had already done and what he proposed to do further. Haile Selassie was familiar with all the facets of his work, he found, and needed no coaching on the significance of the Australian's introduction into the country of such trees as the Mexican pine. In twenty to thirty years this tree attains a growth approximating that which the native eucalyptus and other hard woods acquire only after centuries. The emperor had grasped, far better than his ministers, the asset such forests would prove to be for his people, who so badly needed adequate lumber for housing and for a hundred other uses to which the tough eucalyptus is not adaptable. He was grateful, too, for the successful recommendation of three young Ethiopians for special training abroad in forestry.

Mr. Swain left the palace with a decoration from the emperor, and Haile Selassie's assurance of full governmental co-operation in his program.

Just how effective this pledge was, Mr. Swain discovered in a hurry. Officials who had shown only faint interest in his activities over the preceding twenty-four months all but inundated him with appeals to be told what was needed— and where and when. Furthermore, they produced it. The forestry project underwent a spurt that left him almost dazed at the sudden shift in pace. His office was so jammed with governmental representatives eager to get on with the job that he could hardly find desk room to finish his work on this or that regional plan.

But he grinned when he complained about it.

Then came a blow. Headquarters of the FAO in Rome notified him that contributions by several governments to the United Nations Technical Assistance fund had been reduced, and it would be necessary to cancel some of the programs, in favor of others that would produce the greatest return at the most strategic points. Mr. Swain's was one project that could no longer be financed. The work would have to stop for lack of sufficient money to cover his expenses.

Consternation reigned. The Ethiopians voiced their dismay and their apprehension. Mr. Swain waited. Apparently the newly aroused government administrators channeled the word up to the emperor. Presently a message came back. The forestry program must go on. Mr. Swain's contract would be taken over from FAO by the Ethiopians, and his salary and expenses would be paid from government funds.

The Australian is still at work, and the stretches of pines and other quick-growing trees are still being planted. It marks one of the few instances in which a hard-pressed country managed to salvage an important program from the slashes made necessary by cutbacks at the international level.

Ethiopia will not begin to reap the benefits of the new plantings for some years yet. Gains should be apparent far sooner, however, in the textile field. For the rich soil and the favorable climate have so far been only meagerly utilized for cotton crops. In 1948 only 20,000 hectares were sown, giving a total yield of about 2,000 metric tons. That same year the government requested FAO to send out two specialists to look things over, and to recommend some localities in which rain-grown cotton might be produced efficiently.

In 1952 a third cotton expert was sent, to help in carrying out these recommendations. Better types of seeds were imported and two commercial plots of about 100 acres each were set up as pilot projects. The goal is to make the country self-sufficient on cotton and to eliminate the costly imports, which represent fifty per cent of its annual expenditures abroad. Determined efforts are being made to reach the small farmers, because the growing of cotton is almost exclusively in their hands. In co-operation with technicians of the United States Point Four plan, the FAO men hope to draw in a great many of these farmers by demonstrating to them the improved seeds and methods.

Commercial circles in Ethiopia are very much interested, and are providing valuable support for the cotton scheme. They are lending financial backing as well for development of the Irish flax, in the hope that it will become a substitute for the customary native fibers.

The competition for flax is *musa enset* (false banana), which grows like bananas and looks like them, but produces no fruit. Musa enset is many things to all Ethiopians. Its broad leaves are broken off and used as wrapping for bundles —easily snatched up and as easily discarded. The tough fibers peeled from the stem serve as twine, or are plaited to form a kind of light, strong rope. They can also be woven to make baskets or mats. And the root forms one of the country's staple foods. It is pulped, allowed to ferment for weeks, then cooked and eaten. Such versatility ensures that *musa enset* will continue as an Ethiopian stand-by for years to come, regardless of the introduction of the new types of fiber flax.

The gratifying results of the tests made to date with flax indicate that, with governmental backing, a profitable new industry can be expected to emerge within ten years. There are signs that with proper exploitation the textile requirements of the nation could be at least partially satisfied through the production of linen cloth, and that the treasury could be saved the present drain on its resources through the heavy imports of cotton. But the diversion of the flax crop to the weaving of linen is less likely than the expansion and improvement of the production of cotton, for which the climate and the soil are so adaptable in many parts of the country.

Studies of the imported flax seeds and of the new and finer types of cotton plants are continuing on an experimental farm set up by the government in 1949 at Holletta, about forty-five kilometers west of Addis Ababa. Much of Mr. Millar's work with seeds centered at this farm during his tour of duty in Ethiopia.

Both at Holletta and on his many excursions into the interior, he marveled at the production of wheat and barley in this lush farmland region. But so long as shipment costs for a bushel of grain were the same as for a bushel of coffee, commanding ten times the price, he could foresee no rapid expansion of grain exports from Ethiopia.

While her husband was concentrating on agricultural problems, Mrs. Millar was dealing with the daily routine of homemaking in an alien land. With four children of her own to care for, and few modern conveniences available in her native house of mud and straw—set, as practically all Ethiopian homes are, inside its own compound—Ruth Millar found herself inevitably contemplating another aspect of the impelling needs of the country in which she was a temporary resident.

Repeatedly during each day she spent there, she watched from her doorway the passing of a funeral procession on its way to the cemetery. She learned to identify the stately, colorfully robed priests who, with traditional staffs in their right hands, tapped out the cadence of the jingling musical instruments they bore in their left; and the mourners, always preceded by bearers carrying food for the dead. Quickly she learned to estimate, from the proportions of the casket, the probable age of the deceased.

"There were so many—so many of those processions," she says, "and I came to be more and more dismayed to find that on the average, half a dozen funerals a day were those of small children, or infants. The mortality rate in this age group showed up the terrific need of Ethiopian women for help in the field of maternal and child-health care."

Even before she left Ethiopia with her family, UNICEF had moved into Africa to begin its ministrations for the first time, on a scale that includes most of the continent south of the Sahara Desert. Here the UN teams face the vastness of the region, the absence of transportation, the isolated character of the population in much of the territory and the difficulties posed by the hundreds of native languages. Yet Mrs. Millar is hopeful that the coming years will banish, from Ethiopia particularly, one feature of life there that remains as her most discomforting memory—the necessity of choosing her vegetables and fruits in the open market where, at every turn, she was confronted by mounds of tiny, mummy-shaped coffins, scaled to accommodate the bodies of newborn babies.

FOUR

THOSE WHO HELP
THEMSELVES

MEXICO

FRINGED ABOUT the shore line of a big blue lake in an isolated, mountainous region of southern Mexico lie a score of native villages. Some few dot the islands. Others cling to the slopes of volcanic peaks that rise from the water—the level of which has been sinking slowly and mysteriously for the last several years. None knows why. Together, these communities represent the laboratory for one of the most stimulating experiments on which modern man has embarked.

This is Patzcuaro—taking its name from the lake and from the village now the focal piont of a metamorphosis that began in 1951. In that year the first "fundamental-education" center was established here. Its concept is new and fresh in the field of social welfare. Essentially, it demonstrates that large numbers of persons can be stimulated to rehabilitate their land and their lives, and to evolve through their own efforts into productive workers with higher living standards, if given training and friendly co-operation.

Joint sponsors of the undertaking are the government of

Mexico, UNESCO (United Nations Educational, Scientific and Cultural Organization) and the Organization of American States.

The center itself, situated on a high hill overlooking the lake, occupies "La Erendira," a mansion donated for the purpose by Lazaro Cardenas, former President of Mexico. Its budget in 1952 was $348,600, to which the government of Mexico added $131,000 toward construction and operating costs. Lucas Ortiz, a native Michoacan who for seven years headed his country's booming rural education system, is its director.

All over the globe alert educators register interest when Patzcuaro is mentioned. Relatively few others are aware of its existence. What it is, does and means is best appreciated through glimpses of the impact it has had on the district in which it operates, and on the people there. But a visit involves considerable exertion because the very remoteness of the area 150 miles west of Mexico City—was a major factor in its selection.

Decades, even centuries, have left Patzcuaro untouched by modern civilization. When the era of change began the population was illiterate, malnourished, miserably poor and highly suspicious of strangers. Nocutzepo is typical. The road that leads to it is covered with swirling dust and pitted with potholes, some of them newly mended. Others are under repair. Even a sturdy jeep endures an ordeal of jolting before arrival at the main square.

Surprisingly, a brisk basketball game is in progress on an incongruously excellent court, complete with regulation backstops. The players—lean young Tarascan Indian boys—

are expert, absorbed in their sport.

Bordering the plaza are the same windowless adobe dwellings that have been portrayed interminably in paintings of rural Mexico, with the expected quota of vagrant pigs and donkeys meandering about and men in big sombreros squatting here and there in the shade.

Down one of the narrow alleys between the houses an old well head is visible. Two girls bend above it, pulling up and emptying the same type of earthware jars their great-grandmothers used to lower into its treacherous, tainted water. This community font in its long history has taken a fierce toll of lives. Hundreds of Nocutzepoans have died in recurrent typhoid epidemics without ever suspecting that the water they drank had been the source of their ailments. But its days are numbered.

Just beyond the girls a dozen white-clad workmen are wrestling with stones and cement, oblivious of the sun's intensity. Under the direction of Fernando, a student from the Patzcuaro center, they are laboring to finish a new water tank that will cancel out the old well. Here, as on the basketball court, the atmosphere pulses with animation and energy.

Fernando, distinguishable only because they turn to him frequently for directions, heaves rock and mixes cement as vigorously as anyone. It is obvious that be "belongs." And this to him is as remarkable in its way as the filter and pump they will presently install—gifts from their government—are to them.

Two years ago when he first came among these same men, flaming with eagerness to lend his skills toward improvement in their living conditions, he met hostility and resentment.

They turned away, retreated into their houses and slammed their doors against him and against his teammates.

"We don't want foreigners here—go away!" they had hurled at the strangers, convinced that they had penetrated a disguise of the hated *políticos*, or tax collectors.

Pilar—the only girl among those first students—was equally sternly rebuffed although she had donned one of the shawls worn by native women, and had tried to make friends, to demonstrate to them easier and better ways of cooking and housekeeping. Mothers called their children indoors and told her sharply to keep her distance.

At the Fundamental Education Center, Fernando, Pilar and others dejectedly reported their difficulties. Somehow the faculty members appeared unsympathetic. They merely shrugged and commented,

"It's your problem—solve it!"

They did, in their several ways. Pilar won by persistence, by gently calling a mother's attention to the fact that a child had contracted a cold or other juvenile illness, and by returning again and again with an offering of food for the small patient, or with medicine, shyly tendered. Slowly but perceptibly the ice began to thaw. She was conscious that there were family councils about her. The women sometimes stood silent and hesitant before accepting a proffered gift, but she was patient, and wise enough not to push matters beyond the pace they themselves set. The day came when they invited her into their houses, and listened passively as she ventured tactful hints about the importance of maintaining cleanliness to insure health, or about the good habits children pick up from their mothers.

Since she won her way to their full co-operation Pilar has worked many a small miracle of improvement. She has taught them to boil the water they drink or cook with, because typhoid and dysentery are spread by germs; that soap is a form of disinfectant; and that hens, pigs or dogs should not be allowed in rooms occupied by humans, especially where food is cooked and eaten.

As often as not Pilar conveyed her suggestions in the form of innocently worded questions. Why—she wondered aloud—did they cook over a fire built at the floor level, when a few layers of adobe brick would raise the hearth and eliminate all the back strain involved in bending over the pots and pans? A few tried out the idea, persuading their husbands to obtain the needed bricks, and found it helped mightily. Presently a number of women were following her plan, without any consciousness of prodding from Pilar.

Her next hint proved equally successful. Simple wooden benches for their laundry work, they found, left them much less exhausted because they could stand and move about, instead of kneeling laboriously to the scrubbing. Gradually they began to wait for her further cues.

She did not disappoint them. When she had wangled a tier of shelves for one home, on which to pile neatly the few linens the family possessed, she insinuated a suggestion that a piece or two of native pottery would look attractive on the top ledge. Shortly thereafter not only a simple vase but a cluster of field flowers blossomed there. When in addition a pair of colorful prints appeared on the wall, Pilar knew that two important factors had sunk into their minds—pride in their houses, and a dawning recognition of art in *décor*.

She showed them that even with their limited natural resources, variations in the preparation of food can provide a better diet. For hundreds of years, Nocutzepo and its adjoining communities have raised only one crop—maize. Year in and year out the villagers have lived mainly on the *tortillas* (flat cakes) made from its flour. Long since, the worn-out soil ceased to respond and the yield had grown consistently poorer, while the monotonous diet became a drag on the health as well as on the spirit of the population.

Pilar wooed them into accepting minor changes that have begun to add a bit of zest to their two meals daily. Her first experiment was a timid suggestion that she show them how to make *tortilla* soup, when she came one day upon some of the women grinding their flour, making two pestles dance together in one mortar with the sinuous, graceful movements they had learned from their elders. As a precaution, she brought her own utensils and diplomatically abandoned them as she left, although they had been favorite possessions.

Five or six visits later she daringly proposed a community cooking session, and was pleased when her new friends assented. She tells the story:

" 'We're going to cook with what you bring from your houses. What have you got?' I asked. 'Well, miss,' they said, 'we have *chilacayotes* and *calabash*.' 'All right, we'll cook that. Who will bring the sugar?' One girl volunteered. So we cooked these things collectively, and shared them."

The sugar Pilar mentioned was for the *chilacayotes*—plentiful in Mexico—which they stewed to make the dessert for the communal meal she described. The fruit is light green, about the size of an avocado. The pulp has a melony

67

flavor, and can be eaten either fresh, or cooked.

Calabash is equivalent to squash, and Pilar had a dozen ideas for varying the preparation of this versatile vegetable. She ran through them for the group and they chose to make a recipe still popular in that neighborhood. It was baked, with a sliver of garlic, a bit of sliced onion, a proportion of well-cooked, diced pork and bright wedges of ripe tomatoes, to please the eye as well as the palate. They found it appetizing, and smiled as they tasted.

"That is how I managed to make my way with them," she said. "You know, the women's influence is decisive with their husbands. Later on even the men became pleased to see me and my colleagues of the team as well, and now they accept us and like us very much."

Fernando, a representative of the United Nations Food and Agriculture Organization—which collaborates on the Patzcuaro project—won the friendship of the local people in a different way. He turned to the Tarascans' love of basketball, captured the interest and attention of the boys, and was eventually given entree to their homes and to their families. The court he planned counted heavily in lifting the apathy and inertia that lay like a pall upon the whole region. Gathering at first to watch their sons at work and to make scornful comments, the men found the urge irresistible to take a hand in the venture. Soon the entire village had a new interest and the first real recreation it had ever known. As the word spread, so did the impulse to do likewise. Today there are three or four such courts, and there is a boom on in basketball all around the lake.

The Nocutzepo court was built, as Europeans say, "with

love." Fernando saw to it that the foundations were firmly laid, that the surface was even and that it was smoothly covered with asphalt. For as long as anyone remembered, this plaza had been an eddy of dust in dry weather, and a sea of mud, beloved by the pigs, during the rainy season. Now it is the pride of the community. The idea was Fernando's— but the work was theirs!

Unconsciously, they had put into practice the principle that underlies Patzcuaro. They had demonstrated that by voluntary, co-operative effort, they could change their own lives.

In the last two years, much of what has been accomplished has been the result of that policy of turning leisure hours into some common effort.

The new wells that have made such a difference in their health, have been community projects. And the people who so dreaded tax collectors have learned how to help reduce taxes, as well as to appreciate aid from their own government. For example, a well that was provided by the state of Michoacan in 1951 cost the equivalent of $300, U.S. But at Arocutin in 1952 the people pitched in and built a similar one, at a total cost of only about 350 pesos ($45, U.S.). Both consist of an ordinary hand pump with a deep-well cylinder.

At Jaracuaro, one of the island communities out in the lake, poverty had been the lot of the population for so long that hopeless resignation dominated. Crops cannot be grown because there is insufficient land for cultivation. The waters in which they once fished are dropping away at such a rate that the quay where the canoes used to load is now fifty feet above water level. (The superstitious Indians say that Paracutin is to blame. Paracutin is the new volcano, fifty miles away, that spouted out of a cornfield in 1944. From Jaracuaro its rumble is frequently audible and its smoke visible.)

In recent years these villagers have lived exclusively by the manufacture of straw hats. From practically every house the whirr of an old-fashioned, foot-pedal machine testified to the interminable industry of the family inside. Three sombreros represented a good day's labor by any family, for a net return of about fifty cents per day.

Once established in the confidence of the population, some Patzcuaro students began a study of this situation. Before long they recognized the major difficulties and sat down to talk it over with the natives.

"You have two main problems," they argued, "and if you are willing to make the effort, both of them can be solved. First, you do not earn enough by your work. You are paying high prices for your raw materials—the palm fronds from which these hats are made—and your production methods are uneconomic. Hand labor, and all that. The second is transport. Everything brought here has to come by boat, including food. So you need two things. The first is electric power for your machines. Next you need a causeway across that shallow water, from the mainland, to avoid this cumbersome canoe transport. You can build one. We could show you how."

The villagers, skeptical at first, quickly grasped what was possible to do, and listened intently when the students explained how to go about it. The men organized into groups. Some set about moving the heavy rocks that were to be tumbled farther and farther out into the water from the mainland until they connected with the island, and then filled in with smaller stones and earth to make the road. Some were dispatched to buy the poles for the power lines, and to ferry them across to Jaracuaro, where they were set up in position. "Crefal," as the Tarascans call the Patzcuaro center—from its Spanish initials—undertook negotiations with the government, which agreed to supply the current. The government also sent a tipping truck, on which the bigger stones could be carted to the causeway site.

From the first—even while it was still merely a topic for nightly debate—the plan had roused the islanders and had injected vitality into an otherwise drab existence. As the work went forward anticipation kept pace.

Both the causeway and the electric power are now realities. The day the current was piped in and the first lights flashed on was momentous in Jaracuaro's history—a day of swelling pride and trembling excitement. The climax came at dusk. Church bells pealed, dogs barked, dancers whirled in the streets. At the epochal moment when the lantern in the church tower was due to burst into illumination as the signal that a new era had arrived, all eyes were upturned toward the spire. Those of the youngsters gleamed with expectation. Those of older folk brimmed with tears. Then it came—a glow in the darkness. All voices mingled in the roar of triumph. They had done it—themselves!

Individualists to a man, the Jaracuarans came more reluctantly to the solution of their remaining problem, the price of raw materials. Each little manufacturer persisted in buying his own palm fronds as usual, for the lowest price he could manage. It took more time and argument than the

Patzcuaro students had calculated, to allay their suspicions that by buying as a group, they would risk getting a quantity of inferior fronds, or that their designated "purchasing agent" would certainly make a poorer bargain than they would themselves. They had to be won over one man at a time to the proposal that they pool their resources and buy in wholesale lots, thus benefiting from a cheaper price. Yet at last they came to it, and find that it works very well.

Now in 1954, island existence has a livelier atmosphere. With electric motors to drive their machines, electric irons to smooth the straw, lights by which to work at night whenever necessary and the causeway to expedite transport to and from the shore, labor has been eased, production multiplied, profits increased and life for all in Jaracuaro has a keener quality. Hope lives there.

Of all the villages, however, Patzcuaro students are proudest of Cucuchucu, which had put them to the toughest test of any among the twenty communities. Here the public ways—called streets only by courtesy—were the filthiest, the people the most hostile and the climate the most repellent they had encountered. In some instances the population actually showed violence against the "intruders."

Then came a scourge of typhoid fever. Panic gripped Cucuchucu. The memory of past epidemics during which almost every family had lost someone—a brother, a father, a wife—broke all resistance. When the Patzcuaro faculty and students offered help, either medical or practical, they found themselves warmly welcomed. One of them brought in a microscope and showed the people the evidence that their bad water supply was the source. He outlined measures

Peruvian Indians high in the Andes delightedly greet WHO dusting squads. DDT sprayings protect them, they have learned, against typhus infection, spread by vermin.

Bubonic plague, spread by flea-bearing rats, is endemic in Calcutta. Government cholera control teams, organized with WHO help, fight to exterminate these carriers.

One injection of penicillin, costing fifteen cents, could have saved this Indonesian boy, now permanently crippled by yaws. He is brought to a WHO clinic at Karangasem.

Buddhist priests in Thailand influenced the population to accept spraying of their homes with DDT against malaria, by welcoming WHO teams first, into their temples.

Government health workers in India spray a stagnant pool, to kill malarial mosquitoes. Spectators young and old learn about the importance of good sanitation.

In this jungle setting at Balanzie in the Philippines, WHO nurses administer BCG vaccine provided by UNICEF, during a widespread campaign against tuberculosis.

On a hospital roof in Lahore, Pakistani girls study nursing and midwifery, taught by a WHO-UNICEF international team.

Graduates in midwifery demonstrate for a young Pakistani mother modern techniques in home care of the newborn.

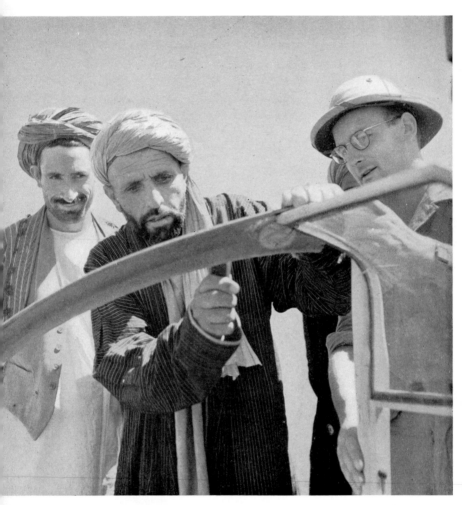

From the sickle to the scythe. Afghanistan farmers are taught by Dr. Martin Sommerauer, an FAO technician, the proper care of new tools to stimulate food production.

"Fish farming," centuries old in China, is being popularized in many countries, adding valuable proteins to deficient diets. A Thailander nabs a big one for supper.

Vast numbers of Ethiopian cattle are being rescued from epidemics of rinderpest by vaccination. Here Dr. R. V. Razmilic, FAO veterinarian, supervises an injection.

Volunteer workers in Emporion, Greece, built their flood control dam by hand, in their spare time. The government paid each a small stipend.

(Top) A partial solution. Underground water sources, located by surveys, are tapped for irrigation or for household use.

(Bottom) Running water comes to Loma de Ramas. The government contributed the pipes. Proud and eager, every villager helped to carry them home—five miles up the mountain.

In French West Africa, education is fascination. These Togolanders are seeing the same UNESCO film-strip—on agriculture—they have seen nightly for three weeks past.

Bolivia has 2,000 lower schools, but only recently built one for these Indian boys at Caroica. While it was under construction, classes were held out-doors.

(Top) Word comes to the Quijano family that a new home in El Salvador's housing program has been reserved for them.

(Bottom) Moving day. The Quijanos take possession of one of 250 tile-roofed brick houses in the Sitio del Niño project.

Scientists are aiding UNESCO in studying ways of reclaiming such arid land as this, in Africa.

that should be taken to correct it. As in Jaracuaro, the people needed only to be told what could be done. They have done it—and much more.

They have a well now in Cucuchucu, assuring clean, safe water for drinking and cooking. There is a basketball field. Various community programs are either complete or well under way. The women not only adopt suggestions made by María Martinez, the home-economics expert assigned to their team, but consult her about further measures to simplify their housework or to promote health for their families. Their affection for her is apparent, and is returned in full measure.

"Anyone whose attitude is patronizing is lost, here," Miss Martinez says simply. "You have to start on the ground floor, forget your own background, and fight on at all costs with a sense of mission."

That she has done. Her efforts were especially fruitful in the matter of the traditional home industry of Cucuchucu, at which these women had worked for generations under conditions which dismayed her. Their products are straw mats called *petates*, woven from a material known as *tule*, which villagers carried home on their backs from neighboring towns. Miss Martinez found that two pesos' worth of *tule* went into each mat, as well as five or six hours of labor. The return was ten centavos an hour, or "practically nothing."

Tentatively she suggested to the women that they could increase their incomes if they would let her teach them to sew and embroider—blouses, dresses for little girls, or tablecloths and other linens. They showed a bit of interest at the mention of possible larger revenues. But. . . .

"First they would tell me, and I would hear them with sadness, 'My hands are hard. I can't use my fingers to sew because matmaking leaves them so stiff and deformed'," Miss Martinez relates. "Or they would say, 'This is my fate. My mother made mats, my father made mats, my grandmother made mats. All of us—that's how we have lived and that's how we will die'."

They found her hard to convince. She had a way of returning to the proposal again and again in the months that followed. Her plan must have been thought over and talked over, and they must have come in their deliberate fashion to a decision that it was worth a trial. For now, with deep but silent satisfaction, Miss Martinez looks around of an afternoon and counts twenty or twenty-five women who come to sit with her, to embroider or sew. Occasionally they mention what they have earned in a week or a month, comparing it with their former incomes from their matmaking toil. Both she and they look quietly content.

"And the phrase 'this is my destiny,' they don't tell me any more, because I won't accept it," she reports proudly.

These have been the victories in the twenty villages. But for each victory there were setbacks, delays and difficulties. The students are quick to concede that they have learned more from their defeats, through their own mistakes, than through their successes. San Gregorio was the scene of a particularly bad one in which Arturo and Juan, members of the same team, figured ignominiously.

The boys had been a trifle over-elated at the progress they had made with Pedro, a small holder of Casas Blancas.

Against his protests that the bitter fruit of a scrawny little crabapple tree at the foot of his garden was "fit only for the pigs, señores," they had persuaded him to let them try grafting on a healthy twig from a pear tree. Weeks later they had returned to Casas Blancas to find Pedro burbling with delight at the prospect of a crop of pears, already indicated by the profusion of delicate blossoms.

This news had of course been wafted around the lake district with the rapidity of a forest fire. Although the area was almost devoid of edible fruit, the simple grafting expedient was unknown there. After its introduction, the students had clear sailing in demonstrating to other farmers how it was done, and in distributing 400 seedling fruit trees obtained from the forestry department of Moralia. (They have also started a nursery of 2,000 trees at the Fundamental Education Center, which will bear several types of fruit, and assure needed variety in the native diet.)

It was on their way back from their second visit to Pedro that the two noted how many swine in the neighborhood were sick and apparently dying, especially the hogs. When they reached San Gregorio they talked about it with the "head man."

"Always it happens, Señor," this official told Arturo sadly. "Every year it happens, and this year it is worse. My neighbor, Sanchez, had ten hogs. Nine have died. Jiminez lost all his stock last year."

"Have you tried to find out the cause?" Arturo asked.

"These things happen, Señor. There are good years and bad years. It is the will of God."

Back at the center Juan and Arturo plotted excitedly.

They were sure that they had recognized the symptoms of cholera in the suffering animals, and that they knew how to deal with it. Flushed with their success with Pedro and the grafting experiment, they felt themselves on the verge of another and more dramatic feat. This time they would tackle a dreaded plague and win further acclaim. Armed with serums and syringes, they scurried off to San Gregorio. One of their professors who had caught the drift of their intentions watched them go, smiling a bit to himself but offering no comment.

Within a relatively short time the boys had rounded up a few "patients" and had one of the pigs securely pinioned. Warned by the squealing of the animals, the head man came bounding upon the two young veterinarians.

"Señor! Señor! What's that in your hand?"

"Just a hypodermic syringe," Arturo told him. "There's no harm in it."

"Let me look. Señor, come here. Let me see this thing."

"It's quite harmless," Arturo insisted. "See this bottle? You remember, when your wife was sick the doctor gave her medicine out of a bottle."

"But that medicine was red, and this has no color."

"That doesn't matter, Señor. This instrument was made to give medicine to your sow. Only instead of making her drink it, we inject it into her blood."

"No! Stand away! If you don't, I'll throw you out."

The two young men, quite deflated, left with the head man's admonition echoing in their ears, "Señores, you are strangers here. We don't need foreigners to show us our business. Now get out!"

And so these two and their teammates, with whom they talked it over, learned their hard but salutary lesson. In widely separated parts of the world United Nations technicians have had to acquire the same wisdom through on-the-spot experiences with the particular prejudices of local people. They have had to grasp the fact that to millions of the earth's inhabitants who are living now almost precisely as their ancestors lived in the eighth or the fifteenth century, the ways of the twentieth century are mystifying and sometimes terrifying; and that for these, the clock can be turned ahead only gradually—never abruptly. Faculty members at Patzcuaro, who deliberately permitted the boys to make their *faux pas*, are wise in their day.

In San Gregorio the setback proved temporary. Eventually Juan and Arturo won both forgiveness and appreciation, and the villagers are only too glad to summon them now at the first sign that the cholera epidemic has struck again.

Their blunder was but one of several the students made. At another village they had undertaken to inoculate the residents against typhoid. While carefully explaining the protection it would afford, they had omitted to mention that each person inoculated would experience a fever for a couple of days. As the patients' temperatures rose, apprehension and resentment kept pace. This time as well, the Tarascans' fright alienated them from their would-be benefactors, and good relations were restored only with time and the exercise of a great deal of diplomacy.

This is Patzcuaro. These are the battles—lost and won. This is the pattern UNESCO hopes to spread across oceans and continents despite lack of funds, time and personnel. In

77

this valley the start was made more difficult through the long isolation of the people and the hardships they had endured for generations. Yet when friendships were firmly established, the students found here the same urge to better their conditions of life as other United Nations teams have encountered in distant regions where they have been eagerly welcomed.

The system of fundamental education has begun to mushroom. A second hub is in operation at Sirs-el-Layan, twenty miles north of Cairo. It was opened and dedicated in March of 1953 by General Mohammed Naguib, as president and prime minister of Egypt. The "laboratory" area that surrounds it is desert, presenting other problems than those of Patzcuaro. Nevertheless the basic challenges of poverty, malnutrition, illiteracy and their offshoots—disease, apathy and hopelessness—remain constant.

Other countries are planning national fundamental education centers, with students drawn from within their own borders. UNESCO and affiliated United Nations agencies will help by supplying experts from various nations.

The need is vast. There are at present about 1,200,000,000 individuals—roughly half of the population of the globe—who are hungry, sick and miserably sheltered, through inability to help themselves. Latin America has millions of them, Africa millions more, and Asia and Oceania as well.

These throngs constitute a threat to peace as well as to one another, unless their situation can be improved. With only modest advances in their conditions of life they could represent the richest and vastest markets yet opened to commerce, and beyond that, a tremendous reservoir of productive manpower and a strategic force for world stabilization.

In the movement toward solution of this vast problem, the contribution Patzcuaro offers is its insistence upon the "team" technique in filling the ranks of the teachers. Of what use is it, this system demands, to send one expert into an underprivileged area to drill pupils in the Three R's, unless they are also given incentives to improve their living standards?

Or again, what does it profit to concentrate upon showing people how to improve their health, if their soil is so denuded that they cannot grow enough food to maintain normal nutrition?

The realistic way, the men and women of Patzcuaro have learned, is to approach the problems from all angles simultaneously—health, agriculture, home economics and so forth—each field of instruction impinging upon the next and supplementing it through community effort, as demonstrated by the teamworkers. An indispensable phase of the plan is the training of native teachers who can in turn teach others, releasing the original squad to begin all over again in a different, equally needy locale.

If it works out according to plan, this spiral will rise consistently, spreading its benefits as each team of students returns to the home country and begins to enlist there still more recruits who will ultimately be sent to new districts to train others. Tens of thousands could be used profitably, but prospects are that it will take years to register and prepare that many.

Patzcuaro emphasizes that it is imperative to begin at whatever point the immediate needs are greatest. Usually this implies concentration upon improving food supplies and reducing health hazards. First the people must be convinced that they can help themselves produce more and better agricultural products, and safeguard their families' health through good water supplies and similar advances. Then the idea is advanced that if they could read and write, they could speed up their forward momentum. Tact and patience are indispensable, but developments around Lake Patzcuaro are proof that the system works.

Although located in Mexico, Patzcuaro draws students from seventeen Latin American republics. Each of the original enrollees was selected by his or her own government because of specific skills already acquired—in public health, home economics or agriculture. Each was, in fact, already experienced as a teacher. Their mission now is to learn how best to teach others to train capable persons in their home countries, so that techniques of self-help can be disseminated even to the least accessible settlements.

Important as it has grown to be, however, the Patzcuaro center is only one detail in the activities of UNESCO. In the great tapestry of the United Nations program of Technical Assistance, UNESCO's task is to direct and supervise all aspects of education, scientific research and cultural interests. It maintains headquarters in Paris. Its annual budget is $8,718,000 (1952) and its staff comprises 850 men and women. Seventy-two nations hold membership in UNESCO.

Under the policy set for United Nations agencies, UNESCO can operate in any country only by invitation, and after a contract has been signed between itself and the government. Part of the funds for the projects are advanced by the governments themselves. The agency concerned pays travel expenses and the salaries of the experts. The beneficiary country defrays their living expenses—stipulated in the contract—in its domestic currency. This procedure evolved because UNESCO funds are limited and, more importantly, because any population reacts with greater pride and interest to a locally supported program than to a "handout" from other nations.

Among UNESCO projects which most directly affect the greatest number of persons are the missions it has sent to assist governments in modernizing their educational systems. Thailand has one of the most fascinating examples, in the educational pilot project housed in a Buddhist monastery at Cha-Choeng-Sao, a provincial capital sixty miles from Bangkok.

Here an international team headed by Thomas Wilson, a New Zealander, began the work side by side with the yellow-robed priests, to the tinkling of the temple bells—leaf bells that sway in the breeze. No living quarters were available for the pupils, but they were quickly provided by adapting some of the classrooms. An old monastery building became the kitchen. Another is now the laboratory. Here the UNESCO group is meeting the challenge of merging old traditions with forms of education that will equip Thai children to meet the gradual incursion of the modern world.

As a preliminary, the government and the UNESCO men had to convince the people that the contemplated training would benefit them, and show them what to expect. The demonstration took the form of fairs throughout the district, which has a population of 240,000 adults and 24,000 children. Kindergarten playgrounds were set up, classroom and arts-and-crafts materials displayed, model farmhouses erected. All facets of the program were explained to and discussed with the rice growers, the fruit farmers, the small industrialists and their families.

Doubt and hesitation evaporated as the spectators began to appreciate the opportunities unfolding for themselves as well as their youngsters. It was immensely reassuring to find that the old ways were not to be discarded, but would remain, parallel with the new. Anticipation replaced uneasiness, and excitement stirred among the older folk as it became evident that they too would be welcome to come and learn.

As things got under way, then, grown-ups worked along with the children. There has been no sudden break with the past and both generations have been pleased as the ancient method of teaching by rote has given way to textbooks. The subjects are the same age-old fables that Thai boys and girls once learned parrotlike and which have taken on new vitality. For these books are illustrated by their own artists, in the Thai's own visual idiom. Paints and brushes—until now unknown to the children—have been brought in and with these and the sand tables on which they build miniature villages, self-expression is encouraged.

Teachers are coming from all over Thailand for the training courses, and taking back many ideas to be introduced into their local curricula. They watch the classroom practice and observe mothers and fathers studying along with their children without self-consciousness. They listen to the teaching—about soap and water and its relation to sanitation and health; about soil and seeds in the surrounding fields; or about forgotten native crafts, happily being revived. They recognize that education can be given through the daily activities of life as well as through textbooks, and that teaching involves both the desire to know and the desire to impart knowledge.

As this book goes to press, UNESCO's staff in Thailand has included Dr. F. C. Kalund Jorgenson, a Danish specialist in language teaching; Professor Charles N. Madge, a vocational-training expert from Great Britain; Dr. Ellsworth Obourn, a United States citizen who is called "the man with the five-dollar laboratory," because he is so versatile at improvising experimental equipment out of scrap; H. C. Burrow of England; K. N. Marshall of the United States; D. C. Smith of Canada and H. H. Penny of Australia. The program is a ten-year one and will be of strategic importance to all the educational reforms in prospect in Thailand, from primary schools to teachers' colleges.

In the field of science UNESCO has established several branch offices to promote international co-operation. It has in prospect a computation center to be founded at Rome, for example. The aim of this center is to make accessible to representatives of countries which could not normally afford such a purchase, one of the great "electric-brain" machines. By using these machines, statisticians, astronomers or mathematicians are able to obtain within a matter of minutes, precise answers to intricate calculations on which they otherwise would be compelled to spend weeks of work, without being quite certain of their accuracy. Four countries—Ceylon, Japan, Italy and Belgium—have ratified the basic international agreement, and the center will be established as soon as six more parliaments have enacted the required legislation.

Indirectly, UNESCO has smoothed the path of learning for millions of students especially at high-school and university level, through an international agreement for removal of tariffs and duties from certain educational, scientific and cultural materials. All countries that have signed this pact undertake to lift prohibitive customs and restrictions from such imports as educational films, scientific or technical magazines and publications, textbooks and like articles which help to spread knowledge. The United States is not among the signatory powers.

One of UNESCO's significantly important projects is a study of "arid zones" which it is sponsoring among scientists in a number of countries. Desert areas across the world are unproductive either because of lack of rainfall, or through man's wastefulness in handling these devastated valleys and plains. UNESCO is helping to work out methods of locating underground or other water sources for these regions. The scientists are studying types of grasses hardy enough to arrest erosion and revive pasturage and are also classifying food plants that might be grown in these zones. They are investigating ways of conserving rain water or of producing more from clouds, and possible methods of drawing energy from the winds or from the sun, as a substitute for electricity.

Conferences on these subjects have been called by UNESCO in co-operation with the governments of Turkey, Israel and Great Britain. To these meetings came twenty-five experts from fourteen countries that have particular interest in the progress of the studies.

UNESCO also initiated another unique project in Mexico which is a boon to scientists and research workers everywhere. In 1951 the agency took over the Cuidadela, the fortress in Mexico City which for over 200 years has witnessed many a martial scene in that country's history, and opened there a Scientific and Technical Documentation Center as a clearinghouse for knowledge.

Every month 1,600 journals, treatises, reports and reviews from every corner of the globe pour into this unpretentious retreat to be catalogued, summarized and translated for the benefit of inquirers of any nationality.

Specialists from one country are thus put into contact with the theories and the work of others, and research which might remain unknown is placed within the reach of all. Each month a bulletin is issued containing a distillation of all the information culled from this mass of scientific documentation. More than 40,000 titles have been listed in the nine bulletins published to date. They are available at cost— with translations into any of eighteen languages—and copies of the originals are supplied by the center, on paper or on microfilm.

Exclusive of the salaries of four experts provided by UNESCO to handle this job, the agency's financial contribution to the center averaged only $10,000 annually over a period of three years. In February of 1954, the institution was taken over exclusively by the Mexican government. UNESCO withdrew completely, and is now launching identical units in India and in Yugoslavia, on the same plan. A fourth will be located in Brazil.

To an average American or Briton it is gratifying to reflect that as citizens of member countries of UNESCO, their individual contributions to this world-wide program amount to only two and one-half cents and tuppence, respectively, per year. The total budget ($8,718,000) is actually less than the city of New York spent ($11,780,470) in the winter of 1947–1948, the year of the big blizzard, merely to clear the snow from its streets.

FIVE

DIARY OF A FIELDWORKER

UNTIL THE discovery that an inveterate man-about-town had crammed his diary with episodes and trivia of life in seventeenth-century London, researchers on that period had been able to produce only unsatisfactory sketches. Samuel Pepys flung the door wide for them. In the process, he demonstrated how illuminating minor details of everyday existence can be, in conveying to those who have never been there and may never go, the atmosphere of any given place.

On the roster of the Technical Assistance program there are hundreds of fieldworkers, among whose obligations is the duty to report regularly and at length about their chores, their travels and their achievements. This they do. The output of these contemporary historians is steady, but apt to be terse and factual. Scientists and technicians are rarely good raconteurs. They write for home-office executives qualified to judge whether a job is being capably performed, and whether or not the funds contributed by the taxpayers of the world are being wisely expended.

Now and then, however, a letter from "back of beyond" smacks down onto a supervisor's desk, and presently a huddle of the entire office staff signals the receipt of the kind of narrative that obliterates time and space. Its readers are transported effortlessly to some hinterland tent or shack where weeks earlier, a particularly articulate expert has tapped his portable typewriter industriously and effectively. Here is more than information. Here is the breath and the color of far lands, the pulse of a country and its people.

Excerpts from two such reports, presented herewith, reflect this faculty for recreating a setting and a situation. They were fished out of the files of two agencies and were written at different times, from widely contrasting locales. One tells of lofty heights, deep snows and bitter cold. It is a soberly phrased summary of a grueling survey trip of three months, through the forests of the high Himalayas.

The other comprises paragraphs dashed off in the tropic heat of southeast Asia over a span of three months, by another Samuel—the same Mr. Keeny who figures in the introductory chapter of this volume.

Dr. Alfred Huber, a Swiss logging expert assigned by the Food and Agriculture Organization to assess the potentialities of forests lying at high altitudes in the mountainous northern provinces of India and Pakistan, sent the first to Rome headquarters of his agency. He made his trip between November of 1952 and March of 1953.

Mr. Keeny forwarded his material to the New York offices of UNICEF, in the course of routine inspections in the field of operations in Thailand, Burma, Indonesia, India, and East and West Pakistan. His travels stretched from December of 1953 to April of 1954.

Let's go along first with Dr. Huber. He wrote thus:

November 30, 1952

"While traveling through the forests of Uttar Pradesh province (India), which march started November 2d and will end December 11th, all the necessary equipment—cooking material, steel cases, camping equipment, maps, survey instruments—and necessary personnel—clerks, porters, mule drivers, cook—with the exception of personal articles such as bedding, blankets, clothing and shoes—has been provided very promptly and efficiently by the Forest Service of Uttar Pradesh. I want to thank for these very good services, Messrs. R. Sahai, Conservator of Forests; D. S. Shiva and D. P. Joshi, Divisional Forest Officers of Chakrata and Tons Divisions, respectively, and their range officers and foresters, who all do their best to make my trip through the high mountains efficient and comfortable.

"I have visited several logging operations in rough country and have been very much impressed by the good job the forest officers and the loggers carry out under the heavy drawbacks and the prevailing conditions. The logging equipment is very limited in quantity and quality, and the personal equipment and clothing of the loggers more than insufficient."

(Further along in his account, Dr. Huber goes into greater detail about this comment).

"This timber is sold to contractors as standing trees. The contractors transfer the logging operation to subcontractors, who themselves pay the loggers in piece work. Thus nobody except the poor logger himself has an immediate interest in improving tools and equipment. These loggers, however— illiterate and poor beyond imagination, guided by many

89

ancient traditions and prejudices, without any communication with the outside world and its technical advancement— cannot be expected to help themselves.

"It may be good to mention one important fact. It will certainly be possible to increase production from these remote forests very considerably. This, however, cannot be achieved by some sort of miracle, i.e., by purchasing and introducing some highly developed machinery, without improving the entire standard of the people connected with the logging operations.

"One of the foremost requirements for any improvement of the present situation is the building of some major road connections and links, to allow motor transportation of mechanical equipment from the railheads to the remote felling areas. At present everything has to be carried on human backs, or mules. Heavy tools, cables for cableways, engines and fuel for them, cannot be transported by such primitive means.

"For this whole month I have been living in the rest houses of the Forest Department. These bungalows are located approximately every six to twelve miles, connected by good mule paths, and in altitudes ranging from 1,000 to 2,700 meters (3,000 to 9,000 feet). They are made for summer use primarily, and lack heating facilities and so forth. Thus we have been very cold in several places, the wind drawing through the cracks and the badly fitted doors and windows.

"This has not been so bad for myself and the accompanying forest officers, but the camp followers such as cook, porters, servants, assistants and mule drivers, who all have to sleep in more or less open sheds, some of the nights at higher altitudes have been most uncomfortable.

"Other, newer rest houses are very well built and offer pleasant accomodations in beautiful surroundings.

"Traveling alone, accompanied by one forest officer only, I have not met any outside person for the whole month, except our camp followers and some occasional villagers. On November 21st, while touring the Upper Tons Valley, six days march from the end of the motor road, I received a letter from Mr. D. Roy Cameron, Chief, Assistance Technique, Rome, designating me as delegate for the second session of the Asian-Pacific Forestry Commission, to be held at Singapore from December 1st to 13th.

"Unnecessary to say that I would be most interested in taking part in this meeting. . . . yet I feel it is not justified to break our journey on the basis of Mr. Cameron's invitation to Singapore only. It takes one week for a porter to carry mail from here to civilization, and ever so many days back. I regret it very much, but the fact of being one-week's hike from the motor road and railheads has complicated this whole matter considerably."

Dr. Huber's rather wistful reference to the meeting he had missed points up the isolation in which he and many of his colleagues live and work. His decision not to interrupt his commissioned undertaking, and to reject what must have been a tempting bid to exchange a frigid mountaintop for a sojourn in colorful Singapore and congenial company, has had many a parallel in the experience of other fieldworkers who have also elected on their own, "not to break our journey" for similarly coveted trips. The project won the toss and the chance was dismissed with the brief notation that "it is not justified," although "I regret it very much."

In the most matter-of-fact way, he sets down immediately thereafter, the essential data of routes followed, places visited and altitudes reached during the twenty-eight days he spent covering the roughest kinds of terrain, by foot or on muleback. Nowhere does he make any mention of physical discomfort.

December 31, 1952

"While hiking through the forests of the two Indian provinces I found that almost all of the modern logging and transportation equipment is completely lacking in these distant areas, although its introduction should be quite easily possible. Logging tools are on a low standard, most of them locally made by some village blacksmith, and consist of axes, saws and some wooden sticks only. Forest roads are chiefly made by hand labor, even rock drilling, and machines for this purpose are lacking utterly.

"The personal equipment of the loggers and forest labor, such as shoes, clothing and protection against cold, rain and snow are of an extremely low standard. It is obvious that without being provided with better clothing and equipment these loggers will not be able to do a much better job than they carry out at the present time. Moreover their quarters, sleeping and cooking accommodations while working in the woods is amazingly simple, consisting of grass huts and branch huts, shelters under rock cliffs, etc. No winter work will be possible under such conditions, although it would be advisable to work throughout the colder season."

In these objective, impersonal observations, Dr. Huber

brings into high relief the key contribution of the over-all technical-assistance program. A highly competent authority on forestry matter is confronted with "axes, saws and some wooden sticks" for felling operations, and with huts fashioned of grass or woven branches. He is mirroring for the Rome headquarters staff the scope of the tasks ahead, before the owner countries will be able to put these timberlands to maximum use and force them to disgorge their unused hundreds of thousands of tons of badly needed lumber. His further notes point the way.

"I contacted several firms in Switzerland, Austria and Germany, and asked for advice from the Forest Research Institute in Montreal, Upper Darby (Pennsylvania, U.S.A.), Zurich, the Swiss Forestry Office in Solothurn and others, with regard to giving me quotations and descriptions of their logging and transportation equipment, personal equipment for loggers, etc. Answers will be added to my final report. I have in mind to recommend a trained Swiss, Austrian or German logging crew to be dispatched to India for a certain time, to demonstrate all such tools, and their maintenance and repair.

"This team will have to demonstrate proper shoes, clothing for mountain logging, proper shelter for winter work (prefabricated, portable huts, including stoves), and sleeping bags. I have been amazed to see that all forest work stops as soon as the first snow falls. In other countries, loggers are waiting impatiently for snow, which is their best means of chuting and sliding logs—by means of snow slides, sleds and sleighs.

"Here no sled has ever been seen, and I shall recommend

experimental work on use of sleighs for log transportation along the existing forest paths, as they are in part well suited to this type of transport. I have found it quite tragic that these people here carry all the timber from high and remote forests to the valleys during the summer months, not taking the least advantage of the facilities provided by the winter snows in areas above approximately 7,000 feet.

"General information. While proceeding through the remote hill areas of the Indian Himalayas, I have seen a tremendous lot of problems, needs and requirements of every kind. These people need transportation facilities, education, help in agriculture, establishment of cottage industries, advice in matters of fishery, medical care—all of this very badly. The problem is not only forestry, and I often regretted not having with me a medical, a fishery, an agriculture and an education FAO expert. All of them would have found a great deal of urgent problems which could be solved or at least supported by FAO and other international organizations.

"Just developing forestry alone will not be sufficient and will not even be possible. Better forest utilization can only be achieved together with other provisions for better transport facilities, construction of motor roads, education of the people, improvement in their agriculture, their cattle breed, their seed stock and their grains. All these improvements have to go hand in hand, and the problem is an integrated one. Thus I feel that FAO should take up the whole matter, not only in the small branch of forestry, and try to help the Indian Central Government in bettering the living and working conditions of these very poor and backward hill populations.

"There is no doubt that there are great potentialities here. The forest wealth is tremendous, the soil very rich and the climate well suited for growing fruits such as apples, peaches or grapes, and the people are very skilled with their hands. But they live in medieval conditions and are lacking all facilities of modern life. The governments (provincial) make a great deal of effort for improvement, but their powers and their means are limited."

Thus Dr. Huber set down his findings, on the eve of his departure for the neighboring mountain forests of Pakistan.

The veriest layman, knowing nothing of forestry, can appreciate the soundness of his analysis and his recommendations for the proper exploitation of these natural resources, and endorse his conclusion that "the problem is not only forestry." He had looked beyond the trees and seen the people. Surrounded by snows and Himalayan peaks, in bitter weather, he was reiterating the same principles that animate the Patzcuaro Fundamental Education Center in Mexico—that the ills that afflict mankind are interlinked and that poor housing, bad health and hunger must be attacked simultaneously.

If additional corroboration is needed, the following notes, extracted from three successive monthly reports compiled by Sam Keeny, will supply it. When he put together the first section, he had just come back to his office in Bangkok after a circuit of Indonesia that had taken two weeks and had included the 1953 Christmas and New Year's holidays. Midway a description of a conference on yaws, for which the directors of the campaigns against the disease in

Indonesia, Thailand and the Philippines had gathered, he wrote:

Jakarta, Indonesia
January, 1954

"Dr. Kodijat (Indonesia) is experimenting with the help of the WHO statistician, on five villages. The results will be available about the middle of the year. Some first results from resurveys suggest that the bulk of new cases do not come from families of infectious cases but from those missed the first time, or from families that had no cases before and presumably got them from contacts in the village, outside the family.

"Dr. Grin (Thailand) suggested that in villages with many yaws, it might be best to give abortive treatments to all who can be reached. Since some people who have no yaws object to treatment, this might reduce the percentage treated to as low as sixty. Dr. Kodijat and his associates seemed more ready to accept this approach than to do family contacts only in the whole campaign. His reasons were:

(1) The cases were found by calling together the village people in the traditional manner. People do not object to this, but many do object to a stranger coming into their homes.

(2) The officials, too, fear that a break in the pattern would cause the people to ignore the assembly gong when it is sounded for other purposes.

(3) It was pointed out that the family do not all come at the same time, some staying at home to look after the animals until the others return. The yaws case is thus often found after the other members of the family have gone

home. To call them back is to 'lose face': doctors are supposed to be infallible in their first judgments.

"As a lay Daniel in a den of professional lions we could do no more than repeat the UNICEF adviser's recommendation and say that UNICEF would be glad to pay for the penicillin to treat contacts, with the dosage recommended by the WHO Expert Committee.

"A field trip was made to the subdistrict of Kedamean, twenty-five miles from the city, to see how the *djurupateks*, high-school boys with three months' intensive training, were doing their job. In the village of Belananredjov (population 1,148) the young man had examined 600 persons and found 136 cases, with an additional 45 contacts. (This was one of the experimental villages where contacts were being treated.) This was a poor village with lots of malaria as well as yaws.

"There is little rice here.

"The doctors were proud that the young *djurupateks* were so alert in picking up yaws cases, and agreed that the youngsters were more accurate than would be young doctors who had seen only a few yaws cases in city hospitals. Their special pride this day was that the *djurupatek* had correctly diagnosed one case, as not yaws, but syphilis.

"While the injections were being finished we wandered over to the heart of the village—a fine old banyan tree in which the spirits dwell. Of course, their real home is on the local Olympus but they come down to dwell among mortals, on condition that they are well treated. And so the banyan tree is hung with offerings of clothing (symbolic and hence small), and the base of the tree is surrounded with flowers

97

and tiny plates of food. The spirits also like a bit of toddy now and then. The families of a young couple just married had brought their offerings in two joints of bamboo, each neatly stopped with a rolled leaf. The villagers regularly express their thanks this way. When the penicillin has done its work (curing yaws) there should be a high old time among the gods under the banyan tree."

Over the Christmas week end Mr. Keeny found himself marooned in an idyllic neighborhood, waiting for the return of officials he was scheduled to see. Friends directed him to a resthouse, where he proved to be the only guest, and made it known to the landlord that he wanted to take a walking trip.

"Here was Arcady," he wrote. "Our little house was perched on the brink of a precipice above a gorge not more than 500 feet wide at the top and half that at the bottom, where gurgled a little river. On the opposite cliff the rice rose in a dozen terraces, dark green at the bottom, but shading into gold at the top. In the village below was a sacred spring, a Hindu temple, and the laundry and bathing place for the village of Manukaja, which was reached up a side gorge by footpath.

"Soon after we arrived a boy of fourteen turned up and announced that his name was Toko. (The word means 'shop' ordinarily, but this was no ordinary occasion.) Toko's English was almost as bad as our Indonesian; but he had an attractive smile, and the manager of the resthouse said he was a good boy and knew the paths to the neighboring kampongs. So he became our guide.

"Next morning we set out for his village. First he took us

to his favorite small temple, which was a tiny shrine thatched with the kind of palm leaves that turn pure black and seem to be reserved for shrines. The walls were ferns twenty feet high, arching inward. The floor was moss in the lovely light green found only in mosses. We understood better than before that the groves were God's first temples and reflected that Toko could not have planned a better visit for Christmas morning if he had known that this was a special holiday for Christians."

At Toko's invitation, Mr. Keeny visited the boy's house, making his way through the inevitable pigs and dogs— "small dogs," Toko said reassuringly—and met numerous brothers and sisters, the title seeming to apply as well to cousins, nieces and nephews. The two visited the bazaar, and later called upon another "family" of about thirty persons.

"Next came a visit to the school—three grades, with 113 children registered. On the list were seven girls, but only one was present. 'Girls no like school,' said Toko. His sisters agreed. It is much more fun to look after the pigs and ducks and to help husk the rice than to sit on a bench from eight to one learning about the absurd things that city children seem to do, according to the *bukku*. Although we were on a holiday, we thought we might learn something about environmental sanitation.

" 'Does the school have a toilet?' we asked Toko.

" 'One o'clock' replied Toko simply.

"We gave up and returned to the resthouse. It was a bit of a shock to come back to the world and to start out on Monday morning, December 28th, even to watch a yaws team at work. But a trip of 200 miles had been planned, and by seven, we were on our way. By eleven, after skirting the lovely shores of south and east Bali, we found the team waiting for us at the back of Bali's highest mountain. The *mantri* (health worker) warned us that the climb to the village where he was to work would not be easy; but we were in a jeep and we insisted on starting. Within a mile the jeep was stuck among the boulders, so we left it and started on foot.

"The going among the lava was a bit rough, but we emptied our shoes of jagged bits of stone from time to time and marched on. Far away was the tourist world of south Bali. Gone were the rice fields. Here was a waste of lava, torn into deep gullies, with only an occasional cocoanut palm growing in stray patches of soil.

"After a few more hot eternities we finally reached the poorest village we've seen—and that includes India. But their welcome was none the less gracious for that. The *mantris* had been there nine months before and were old friends. The roll call brought many a cured case, happy to show the healed scars. But the village was a scattered one and many had been away at work, so that there were still plenty of cases to be treated. The head man and his son helped organize the queues and brought the shyer ones forward. All was good will—and trust. Here on a barren mountain, looking down on the Java Sea, these people had no trouble in understanding—and appreciating—the United Nations."

Learning that the two *mantris* would be busy until evening and might have to spend the night in the village, Mr. Keeny, "thinking of the hundred miles of bad roads ahead and of the yaws school still to be visited," left them and began the hard scramble back down the mountain. By two o'clock he was back on a narrow dirt road that follows the shore of the Java Sea. Shortly thereafter he reached the home of a district officer and was given the opportunity to wash away some of the lava dust he had collected on his climb.

"Clean, cool and tidy, we were now ready to visit the yaws school, to which come the trainees from all of the Lesser Sundas. There we found a dozen young men, mostly from Lombok, the next island to the east. (The workers for Bali itself had been trained in the previous group.) There were also present a *mantri* and an assistant from the Indonesian part of Timor, at the eastern end of the chain. They showed their origin by their darker skin and curly hair—the mark of the Polynesian.

"The Timor *mantri* was one of the most intelligent we had met, and we had a fascinating hour with him on the special problem of reaching the people of Timor and the smaller islands off its coast. (Headquarters may look forward to requests for outboard motors suitable for driving local craft.) That they should be reached—and soon—was shown by the *mantri's* sample figures. Of some 2,000 children he had examined in a dozen schools, more than half had yaws."

Before he began work on his report for the following month, recording visits to Burma, East Pakistan and India, Mr. Keeny had collected a few more interesting facts about the yaws campaign in Indonesia. One was that 63,000 cases had been treated during January. The other, that the complete cost to the Indonesian government and UNICEF for examining ten persons and treating one case, is down to

$1.00, of which UNICEF pays thirty-five cents.

Rangoon, Burma

February, 1954

"Our first call was to talk about the antimalaria program, which survived parlous days last year and protected about 1,000,000 persons. This year the target is 2,700,000, and all the DDT is already in the country, or on the way.

"Everything is ready 'except for some final arrangements in the Shan States.' We congratulated our colleagues for their handling of a little legitimate hijacking—the way in which they had held a river boat until the barges had delivered the DDT from the ocean-going steamer that had brought it. With initiative like this, and a bit of luck, they are on their way to success in the third year of their five-year plan. The government officials assured us that they will buy the 416 tons they need to match the UNICEF contribution to date. We emphasized that the DDT must be bought by the end of March if it was to arrive in Rangoon by the deadline in November. Supply lines are worrisome things.

"Next came the BCG (antituberculosis) program. We were lucky to get the final comments of Dr. Kvisselgaard, who was leaving that night after winning—with ten per cent to spare—a terrific struggle to test 1,500,000 children under circumstances that would have discouraged anybody except a young Dane. He leaves behind him ten organized teams and an enthusiastic Burmese team leader determined to keep up the tempo of the campaign.

Dacca, East Pakistan

"The MCH (Maternal and Child Health) building is no longer a pile of bricks and mortar, but a humming center filled with Moslem mothers *in posse* and *in esse,* and with children whose black eyes look even blacker from the kohl with which they are decorated. One of the center's many problems is what to do with visitors who come from outside the demonstration area. We recommended—flexible boundaries.

"While we pondered this question, the UNICEF 'school bus' rolled up. Somehow, we had expected to see a dozen or so trim little trainees come tripping out. Instead, there appeared a stately stream of hooded ladies, each seemingly more pregnant than the other. We did not wait for the last!

"UNICEF's biggest program in East Pakistan is that against malaria. Last year only 1,700,000 people were protected; but this year the goal is 3,000,000. DDT and sprayers are in place, except of course some spare parts which we were asked to ship by air. This last-minute call is practically *de rigueur* with all malaria programs and was made with the customary apologies. We replied with the standard lecture on the costs—and took the specifications. They will have the spare parts in two weeks.

"Although the campaign will be twice as large as last year's, the local budget is a bit smaller. This piece of magic will be accomplished by borrowing staff from other projects—and passing on the costs to the districts. There is no force for decentralization like necessity.

"This project budget is but a sample of East Pakistan's economic plight. The whole public-health budget for this disease-ridden 45,000,000 persons amounts to just under $1,000,000—or two cents a head per year!"

As his later references to this predicament reveal, the

"two cents a head per year" for all health measures plagued Mr. Keeny from then on, in nightmarish fashion. He explained at length to his New York headquarters, the whys and the wherefores.

"Times are hard because jute prices have been low. Then acreage was cut to lift prices. Now the prices are still low, there is less to sell, and the new crop is three months away. Even the money that is in the country is hard to get into government coffers, for the tax farmers who raised the money under the Zamindar system have mostly fled to India (after partition) and new attempts at taxation are still pretty feeble.

"This situation is most serious for the future of the fight against malaria; for two thirds of all the people who suffer from it in all Pakistan are here in this crowded province. But no matter what the consequences, apparently the budget for antimalaria work won't be more next year than this, and that won't buy more than half the 300 tons of DDT being used this year. As this brutal fact sank into our mind, we suddenly saw that our shiny new plant at Nowshera won't be much help if East Pakistan can't buy the product (DDT locally manufactured).

"Somehow the program for 1955 will probably be salvaged—but what about 1956? And always in our mind are the other 10,000,000 beyond the 3,000,000 already protected, who live in highly malarious areas. We are left with the unwelcome conclusion that unless Central Government makes grants, or subsidy from international sources is found, East Pakistan will keep on shivering from malaria for many years."

He seems glad to go on from there to more cheerful news.

"When darkness fell, we opened office in our room in the new hotel, the chief artistic decoration for which was our ash tray—a tin can that had seen better days. Here came Sister Benedict to learn of the fate of her request for equipment for her hospital, now up to the beginning of the second story. We were happy to tell her that she might call on UNICEF for what she needed—up to $25,000.

"There too came Dr. De Marchi, the enthusiastic TB expert from Italy supplied by WHO. Within one year he has started from nothing—or less—and built up a clinic that has nearly 9,000 attendances a month. The patients like him and his staff, the government is happy about his work, and we were delighted to hear that Italy has agreed to let him stay another year. We talked until midnight about his plans for extending his work to the smaller towns and the villages.

" 'The people are ignorant and shy and will not come to us early enough; we must go to them,' said Dr. De Marchi. We hope Headquarters will agree, and that he will have no trouble in getting equipment for the two new centers the government has sanctioned, plus a small portable X-ray that can be moved by jeep or by boat in this watery land."

Delhi, India

"The next morning we reported to the little palace of Patiala House, where WHO and UNICEF work peacefully together on their joint projects. The atmosphere was happily changed from that of our visit a month ago. Then, five State MCH projects involving nearly $1,000,000 worth of international aid had been stuck for months, because Technical Assistance could not provide enough money for personnel.

After a December session (with provincial officials) we cabled to Headquarters, with faint hopes, a proposal to break the deadlock. Whether the Christmas spirit had softened them we shall never know, but the answer had been the right one. Gone was the frustrated philosophizing about how the UN should have been organized. Now there were confident reports on plans of operations mailed, supply lists completed and staff recruited. Special thanks are due to the Colombo Plan (British) for supplying the staff, and to Dr. La Rue of WHO for his energetic help."

On his way back to Bangkok, Mr. Keeny must have been comforted by the impending opening of the five new centers, whenever his thoughts about the situation in East Pakistan grew too depressing. His March tour took him to the western half of that strangely bisected land.

Karachi, West Pakistan
March, 1954

"First we visited the Holy Family Hospital, which UNICEF is assisting with training equipment for its maternity work. We wanted to find out whether the hospital really existed now. We found the three-story building not only had a roof on but that taps, when turned, spurted water. In a back room we even found a new X-ray in crates, and beside it, a small nun with a Virginia accent. She said that she had put X-rays together before. We told her where there were some technicians in the city, working with the same type of machine, but had a feeling as we left that before long she would probably be helping them—instead of vice versa!

"Soon after we left the hospital we passed one of the refugee settlements on the edge of town. These are built of mud and matting, reinforced with tin cans and string. Unfortunately there had just been a heavy rain and the settlement was not at its best. The entire place was a sea of muddy water some six inches deep, which nobody seemed to like except the inevitable small boys, who, the world over, like to feel mud squirting between their toes. For the housewives the outlook was less cheerful; walls were melting, the matting hanging in the water and the furniture—if any—soaked. We recollected a recent reminder from Headquarters that we should be careful about going too far with maternity facilities because 'the normal delivery should take place in the home.'

"Coming as we did from Bangkok, we naturally thought that a nice lot of water ought to have ducks on it and some fish in it. Since it rains only a few times a year in Karachi, we dismissed these thoughts as impractical and set out for the desert site where the TB convalescent center was said to be under way.

"When we got there, we were astonished to find some 200 workers—mostly women—of course—building walls, some of them to enclose X-ray rooms to house UNICEF equipment. There will be 225 beds at least. We inquired of the director whether there would be money for the staff, as well.

" 'Oh, yes,' he said. 'Of course the salaries aren't much, and not everybody is willing to spend twenty-four hours a day in a TB camp in a desert, with the bright lights of Karachi clearly in sight fifteen miles away. It's only half an hour to town and there is no bus. Now, if UNICEF. . . .' "

Mr. Keeny's final session in West Pakistan concerned

the antimalaria campaign there. He found it slightly better than in the eastern half of that country, with 1,000 tons of DDT on hand or on order for this year's spraying—enough for 10,000,000 people. Six million were protected there last year, and "we shall settle for 8,000,000 this year."

Before midnight that night he was on the plane to Cairo, from which he headed westward for a conference in New York.

"Usually we waste no time getting to sleep," he recalled, "but we couldn't get East Pakistan out of our mind: 20,000,-000 people, for whom malaria is the most feared disease. We remembered the stories of Gregory, in our Bangkok office, who told of the old days in East Pakistan when many a village couldn't round up enough hands to harvest the jute. Two cents a year for all public health. Protection is cheap, but not that cheap. And yet the experts say that no country, however poor, can afford to have malaria. Perhaps the price of jute will rise; perhaps they can raise some taxes, after all; perhaps Karachi will help; perhaps they can do their own spraying; perhaps. . . ."

These are the problems. These are the people who work at them, and worry about them. Together, they explain the existence of the United Nations program of technical assistance, in which FAO and WHO are integral units, and UNICEF an indispensable "extra arm."

SIX

BY THE SWEAT OF
THEIR BROWS

KOREA AND GREECE

IN SOUTH KOREA in the spring of 1953, life in the native villages was quiescent and the population numb, as though rousing from a nightmare. The tide of battle had long since rolled northward and had arched raggedly across the thirty-eighth parallel, where the front line alternately buckled and firmed again, as United Nations and Communist forces slugged it out in the desperate weeks that preceded the truce agreement in July.

On splintered trees that had survived bombs and artillery duels as opposing armies advanced, retreated and advanced once more, nature was signifying disdain of man's inter-ference with the enduring cycle of the seasons, by putting forth a few brave buds. Even in the trampled and denuded shrubbery, spikes of tender green swayed like miniature banners.

As resilient in their way as their tough little trees, the South Koreans marked these harbingers and called upon their own reserves of strength to cope with the tasks that faced them. They had endured a rigorous winter, aggravated by their lack of sufficient clothing, food or fuel. Families were scattered and local populations decimated by the tragedies of war and by exposure to bitter weather, disease and malnutrition.

Months earlier, the ships of friendly nations had begun to reach these coasts, bringing cargoes of emergency relief supplies. Advisers from abroad had launched surveys of the devastated national economy to work out rehabilitation plans on a vast scale with representatives of the government of the Republic of Korea. In the main their activities concentrated on the larger cities and towns. The rural areas were less aware of them, or of the efforts under way by the Rhee administration in co-operation with the United Nations Korean Reconstruction Agency. More and more frequently, Army engineers and technicians in uniform who had first grappled with such problems were being replaced by civilians, as the military moved outward and onward, and the thunder of the big guns grew fainter in the distance.

What little they were able to do with their slender resources to restore their rice paddies and farms, the Korean villagers had accomplished. Now the slack season was at hand, and employment tapered off as usual almost to nil, while the farmers waited for warm weather to ripen their plantings. Meanwhile their incomes diminished drastically. Food was hard to come by, and as rations lessened, physical energy dwindled in proportion. Men, women and children moved ploddingly, sitting down frequently to doze in the sun.

Then something out of the ordinary happened. It began when a jeep rolled into one of the villages in Chollo Pukdo province, and out stepped three strangers. The first unmistakably was a Korean—a government interpreter. The others were Americans, in mufti. Casually the trio strolled over to a man perched on a box in the town square, and struck up a conversation with him about conditions in the community. They seemed particularly interested in the labor market. Presently a knot of townsfolk gathered, eager to discuss their situation and their enforced leisure. Only one or two shopkeepers, it developed, had anything resembling a steady income, and even they were hard pressed to keep their families provided with bread.

Everything the Koreans had to say was corroborated by their seedy appearance as they clustered about the new arrivals. Without exception they were painfully thin, their brown faces drawn and peaked. Their garb was nondescript. It consisted of tattered native jackets and trousers combined here and there with bits of old American uniforms acquired somehow, to help repel the cold. One or two wore battered leather shoes. The rest had wrapped their bare feet in sacking, tied on with rags long since stiff with grime. Yet they showed no tendency toward self-pity, but rather relief that they still had breath and life, after the horrors through which they had come.

Through the interpreter, one of the Americans put a question. What did they raise as a main crop? His query seemed to disconcert the natives. No one seemed to be very certain on that point. It was not exactly easy to explain, they stammered. The questioner looked puzzled. Then a crippled old villager, hobbling forward on tottery ankles, thrust his bearded face between the shoulders of two younger men and piped up,

"Why—everybody knows we raise barley, here!"

With embarrassed, apologetic smiles and significant gestures toward their temples, the rest of the group conveyed that the newcomers were to pay no attention to the old fellow because he was a bit touched in the head. Nobody actually contradicted his statement.

In English, in a quick aside to his companions, the Korean interpreter explained that the old man had been tactless. Any Korean village with a sense of local pride prefers to raise rice, he murmured, and will try to conceal the fact that it does not. Barley, he added, is looked on as a plebeian crop.

Taking the hint, the American shifted the conversation. Had any of those present, he wondered, any suggestions for improvement of their village? Now the responses came quickly and enthusiastically. There was the water gate which controlled the flow of irrigation water for their crops, and which they had often talked about widening. But they had no funds, nor the prospect of any. Some day when they could get enough money together, the village was going to buy some cement and widen that water gate. It would then be feasible to increase the acreage they were able to cultivate, and they would not only have enough food, but would also be able to sell their surplus.

An excellent prospect, the Americans agreed. But wasn't there another project that could be handled with exclusively local materials, on which they could all work together during these weeks of idleness, to improve their community?

At this point the village elder took over, with a gleam in his eye. The suspicion was dawning on him that these Americans had in mind a bit of financial help for the town. He reiterated that the greatest benefit would come from the water-gate widening. Cement they must have, he said firmly: about 600 bags, he calculated.

The strangers came to the point. The Korean government, they told the assembled men, was anxious to help villagers like these help themselves. It was even prepared to pay them a tiny wage each day, if they would volunteer their services to complete some program that would be of mutual benefit for the people. But the government was not willing to pay for any materials, therefore whatever was planned must be carried through with their own resources.

Excitement flared among the villagers at this news. Of course, if their government wanted their help, they would all work! Yet the talk kept circling back to the water gate as their outstanding need. The unofficial mayor dropped his estimate, cautiously, to 300 bags of cement, and then to 100 bags. The Americans kept on shaking their heads. Cement could not be bought locally, therefore another project must be chosen. The villagers would not have it so.

"After all," they challenged their spokesman, "it can be done without cement. The main thing is the digging. We can shore up the banks with stones, and they will hold. Let's work on the water gate."

So the village elder reluctantly abandoned his insistence on the cement. The whole group, now imbued with fervor, moved off with their new acquaintances to have a look at the water gate and to show exactly what they could do, and how they could do it. They pointed out just where the additional water would be directed into the new fields, and estimated how many man-days of work the task would require as well as how many acres would be added to their holdings.

Everyone stood solemnly about while the Americans produced official-looking forms, which were filled in then and there with the agreed figures, with the help of the interpreter. They all witnessed the transactions as the papers were signed—by the Americans on behalf of the government of Syngman Rhee, and by the local leader on behalf of the village.

After that the American spokesman took from his jacket pocket a wallet generously crammed with *hwan*—the Korean currency. Rapt, the villagers watched him count off 12,000 *hwan* and put it in the hands of their leader. Out of this fund, the Korean explained, each man was to be paid every evening as his day's work was finished, until the entire job was completed. They were now partners with their government, which had provided this money.

Still aglow with their plans to pool their efforts in the community project, the villagers plied him with questions. Why should their government pay them, when they were willing to do this work in their spare time? After all, they were patriotic and willing, and their government could have their services for nothing. Their faces conveyed their politely unspoken thought: "There must be something fishy about this!"

The Korean did his best to explain. The government felt that those who worked should be paid, he said. Otherwise, some who preferred to sit back and to take it easy might jeer at the laborers for contributing their toil, when the lazy as well as the workers would eventually benefit. If men who donated their services were assured a slightly better income, the slackers would be silenced and the whole community would be helped.

At the same time, the interpreter added, the work they had contracted for would produce larger crops and more food for everyone. This in turn would mean that they could feed themselves in future seasons, rather than remaining dependent upon what limited relief stores the national administration could send them. The government would of course save money to that extent, since many villages were adopting identical plans of self-help.

The Koreans listened intently. It was only too evident that the whole thing had occurred so abruptly that they could not absorb its details, without thinking it over and talking it through. The visitors climbed back into their jeep, pointed it back the way they had come, and drove away with assurances that they would be back within a couple of days. Behind them, the townspeople looked at the money in their leader's hands, turned incredulously to look at the water gate again, and scratched their heads. They must have been swindled somehow, they agreed—but how? They had the 12,000 *hwan*, and the money was good. It wasn't much, but it would buy a bit more food each day for their families.

Confusedly, they pondered the riddle. All they had pledged was to do something which would help themselves, and they had been willing to do it without pay! The discussion went on until one man pointed out that the day was still comparatively young, and that there was nothing to prevent them from getting a good start on the project that had roused such hopeful prospects. They scattered in all directions, in search of their tools.

Two days later, when their newfound friends arrived back at the scene as they had promised, the villagers clambered from their ditches to point out proudly that they were well ahead of their schedule with the work. More than that: they had been talking things over and had decided to continue to use their spare time to complete two or three other local improvements before the farm crops claimed their labor once more. They knew exactly what their next project would be. They would build a stone wall in the form of an arc, at one edge of the village where the wind had for years swept sand into the houses and streets, blinding passers-by and piling up against walls. After that they would deepen the village reservoir, which had never been entirely adequate for their needs.

This time the visiting trio did the listening. They approved the plans without argument, for the villagers made no mention of any material that was not at hand. The site of the future wall was inspected, and also the reservoir, and two additional contracts were promptly written up and signed as before. Once again a sheaf of *hwan* changed hands, and everybody beamed all around, as the strangers left. One village in Chollo Pukdo province was a far different place than it had been two days earlier, and the cost to the government was insignificant.

The men in the jeep did not stop with that one village. They spent six weeks during April and May of 1953, making dozens of such calls, inspecting scores of canals, bridges, reservoirs and fields. They made no suggestions. They simply presented the possibilities inherent in the government's offer, and waited for the villagers to come up with the ideas and the leadership which invariably emerged. They were adamant on the point that only local materials be used. And they signed a score of similar contracts, always handing over the estimated total of the wages involved, sometimes on the same day that they arrived in a community and arranged for the volunteers.

In several instances they found that the population longed for a larger or a deeper reservoir, as insurance against drought. In others they found coastal fishermen dreaming of a saltern, without realizing that they could easily have pooled their labors and built one for themselves. (A saltern is a large, shallow depression into which the Koreans draw salt water from the sea, then drain it out and collect the residue of brine, to preserve their catches of fish.) In the past, quantities of fish have been allowed to spoil because salt is difficult to obtain. Each fishing village that acquires a saltern thereby immediately expands its income as well as its own food supply.

Whether it covered the repair of a broken bridge, the extension or widening of canals, the building of stone abutments or the digging of a saltern, each contract represented progress brought about by local labor, with local materials. It also forecast an increase in the ability of the population to get more out of their fields or their fishing grounds. No other type of contract was approved.

To have relaxed this rule, says the man who gave it its start, would have upset the movement and put it on quite a different basis. Perhaps it is time that he was introduced, for he is the man in the jeep—the one who directed the conversations with the villagers, and who signed the first contracts on behalf of the government. He is Glen Leet, a specialist in community development organization for the United Nations Technical Assistance program, and he was in Korea as a fieldworker on loan to the United Nations Korean Reconstruction Agency, usually called UNKRA.

Mr. Leet is eminently qualified to comment on what happened in his particular phase of the rehabilitation work in Korea, having been one of the United Nations representatives who originally sold the Greek government on an identical plan. It was, in fact, so successful in rural Greece that its features there are gradually being disseminated to other nations through documentary films, and through newspaper and magazine articles.

In Korea, the scheme worked simply, as it had in Greece.

"Naturally, the government of the Republic of Korea had to get the funds from outside its borders," Mr. Leet said, "since it was just about bereft of any resources of its own. What happened was that the Rhee administration took the grain from the ships sent in there from other nations, and sold it to the needy people at a very nominal price, which kept the recipients from feeling that they were accepting international charity. The income from the grain, of course, was clear profit. It did not represent any vast resource, but it was enough to allow the government, in co-operation with UNKRA, to set up this plan of paying out the fund in the form of a modest daily wage to volunteers, if they would devote their spare time to community rehabilitation.

"Any such improvements would benefit the nation as

well as the village. But the money would not have lasted very long if large proportions of it were to be spent for scarce materials, which would have had to be imported from some other part of the country. In any case, transportation problems in Korea would have made that impractical. Immediate action would be possible, however, and the work would be done if it depended only on materials already at hand. And that's how we worked it."

The only surprise Mr. Leet experienced in Korea was the fervor of the patriotism the people displayed. He had had experience in Haiti, Ecuador, Egypt, Syria, Turkey and Lebanon as well as in Greece, but nowhere had he encountered a population so alert to any suggestion that their country needed their help, or so grateful for the chance to offer their service.

Neither in Korea nor in the other countries was there lack of ideas or of leadership. Invariably someone in every community had dreams of betterment for his people and himself, and confronted with an opportunity to see them realized, would surge to the fore with his plan and carry his neighbors with him.

That's the way it was in Korea. That's the way it was in Greece, in those remarkable eighteen months when nearly 1,500 isolated, desperately poor villages caught the spirit of the plan broadcast to them by their national government, and began a crusade of self-improvement that continues today as a vital force in Greek life. The start was made in 1950, with an explanatory circular drafted by a United Nations adviser and dispatched by the Greek government to all provincial governors. Financial help was provided there by the United States Economic Co-operation Administration—the Marshall Plan. The United Nations made available the technical assistance teams. The Greeks contributed the greatest asset—hundreds of thousands of hours of voluntary labor which, if paid for at the normal wage, would have made the costs of the projects prohibitive.

Mr. Leet, who spent six years in Greece as the head of a welfare mission first sponsored by UNRRA and later by the United Nations, likes to recall what happened in the village of Demestica, renowned throughout the country for the excellence of its wine.

Demestica boasts only forty-five families, and is perched high in the mountains of Achaia, in the Peloponnesos. It was almost inaccessible, the nearest road lying some seven miles distant. To reach it meant a hard scramble over a rugged mountain path.

Transportation over that difficult trail of the fine, sweet grapes the Demesticans raised, had never been possible. So they depended upon a primitive wine press, imported years earlier, to do a crude job of pressing out the grape juice. It was then sent on muleback to the winery, more than twenty-eight miles distant. The cost of such freight was high enough to leave the vineyard workers only a slight margin of profit.

For years they had sighed for a real road to link their community with the one that lay across the brow of the mountain, and had computed mentally, time after time, how much such a road would add to their earnings. Yet decades went by, and nothing changed.

Until, one memorable week end, an uncle of the mayor

came huffing and puffing up the trail. He brought a bit of news that set up a buzz among the men who sat chatting and sipping their strong black brew in their usual haunt, the village coffeehouse. The visitor, a lawyer from Patras, told of the arrival of the government circular, and of the offer it brought of a small daily payment to each volunteer, if the people of any individual village would agree on some common project and use their spare time to complete it. The wage was to be only 11,000 drachmas (about 73 cents) per day. Tools, materials and labor would have to be furnished by the villages.

In no time at all, after the hubbub of questions and exclamations had died away. Demestica had organized for the plan to which all minds turned—the road! The road they must have! A committee comprising the mayor and a couple of older citizens left the same day to go to Patras and to make all arrangements. The matter was laid before the provincial governor, who conceded that it was an admirable objective. He suggested that it would take time to get the funds to them, and that they go back and wait.

They went back, but wait they could not. Everyone was now too impatient. It did not matter that the government could supply no engineer to advise them, nor that they would need dynamite for some of the rockier outcroppings that must be cleared, and that they had no dynamite. Picks and spades were assembled, and scouts were sent out to plot the most logical route for the workers to follow. Meanwhile two men were sent to the Claus Wine Company, which handled their grape juice, to ask whether the company would not lend them some dynamite, and a man who knew how to handle it.

The proprietor of the wine company was more than willing. If his trucks could reach the village the expensive mule-back transport could be eliminated. Thereby he, the vineyard owners and the workers would all make a bigger profit, because his equipment could extract more and better grape juice than their old-fashioned wine press. He sent the dynamite and the dynamiter within the next few days.

The work went forward consistently. Sometimes only six men could spare the time for it in any single day. Sometimes there were thirty-five. The farther it stretched, the faster it went, as the fever spread and more villagers—even the women—rushed to help.

On that stony ground and with only hand tools to do the job, the road was not the smoothest or the finest ever built, but to the villagers who had made it a reality, it was superb. And over it, on September 14, 1950, came chugging a station wagon carrying officials from the ECA, the United Nations and the Greek government.

It was the first motor vehicle ever to reach Demestica. The children swarmed, clamoring just to touch it. Their elders, who had worked frantically to clear the last rough stretch so that the station wagon might drive on into the town, produced a guestbook and to commemorate the arrival of the only foreigners to set foot in the village in its entire history, had the visitors inscribe their names and the eventful date.

The guests were entertained in the home of the mayor, to which the Demesticans streamed to talk about the tremendous thing that had happened, and of how much the road would mean to them. They brought out walnuts and tempting fruits which they had always raised, but had never been able to market. Now they could, having access to other towns. They had never had a school, but it might now be possible to get a teacher to come. Above all, they could double the 250 acres of land they usually cultivated, since crops could be trucked out with relative ease, for sale in the countryside.

One of the United Nations men asked what the road had cost, in wages. The villagers knew exactly. They had collected from the government 13,000,000 drachmas, the equivalent of $787, or $79 per kilometer (five eighths of a mile).

"But you can't build a mountain road for so little!" exclaimed the surprised official.

Nevertheless they had. Everyone had contributed ten days of work to make it possible. They went on to make a rough calculation of the amount of produce they would now be able to transport, and found that the savings in truckage costs in less than one season would more than cover the total expense of the new thoroughfare! That was fine, said the visitors, but what would become of the people who had made their living through transporting the grape juice on mules?

"How do you suppose we are going to have another thousand *stemmas* (250 acres) cleared for cultivation if the mules and their drivers don't work on it?" the Demesticans retorted. "There will be plenty of work here for both men and animals for a long time to come."

So it has proved. The men of Demestica no longer pass

their months of idleness as they used to, just sitting about in the coffeehouse. They are too busy with the extra work that has opened up, especially since the new road was still further improved by a bulldozer sent up by the wine company owner, to level it off firmly. Their produce is going to market steadily, and the average family's income is substantially increased. They have a community radio now, that brings news of the outer world. Relatives and friends come far more often to see them, and the life of the whole town has been enlivened and enriched.

It is true that professional engineers who have come to inspect their road have been critical. These experts have pointed out that bridges should have been installed at three points where the villagers had simply packed gullies with dirt, and that spring rains would wash away these fills. The Demesticans have remained placid. They had foreseen that the fills would wash out, and that they would be isolated again at intervals. But for nine months in the year, they knew, they would have practically no rain, and when the seasonal floods did come, it would take only about three hours of communal effort to fill in the gullies once more. The bridges would have cost approximately $1,000—which they did not have. They could keep the road intact for all but about two weeks annually. After decades of seclusion, they were well content to be cut off for a short while from the outside world, if they could reach it easily during the remaining fifty weeks each year.

They felt a sense of participation, too, as they gathered each evening to hear the news broadcast over their radio through the government network, describing activities in neighboring places no larger than their own. Sometimes they picked up ideas that could be applied locally. In any case, it was pleasant to feel themselves qualified to comment about such programs, adversely or favorably.

Ever since the movement began, the government radio commentators have had plenty to report, first about specific plans and later about results obtained. The Demesticans heard about the drainage project in Bisdouni, for example, which they knew was about the size of their own village. There the people had chosen to widen and deepen an already existing drainage ditch, even without fully appreciating the chain of benefits that would ensue. It had been expected that the work would hasten the draining off of rain-drenched land by a few weeks, and these anticipations proved correct. The plowing season thereafter began earlier. The surprising thing was that even the few weeks gained brought prosperity above and beyond the calculations of the Bisdouni residents, because corn could now be grown where none had grown before.

Over their radio, too, the Demesticans heard about another, shorter road that was built by the citizens of Kalamos, in northern Attica. It extended only six and one-half kilometers (just under four miles), but it connected Kalamos with a little port on the Saronic Gulf. This gave the people access by boat to the adjacent islands, where they found a much larger market for their citrus fruits, as well as cheaper fish and olive oil to meet their own needs. Soon thereafter, they could report with understandable pride that the sale value of land in Kalamos had risen to correspond with this newly gained access to the surrounding region.

It was fascinating to hear about the resources village inhabitants discovered within themselves. And the variety of the undertakings kept pace with their growing numbers. The reports kept coming. About Lavrion, where the people tackled the completion of an abandoned dock foundation, and opened up a cheap route to Athens for their island farm products; about Peli, where 500,000 trees were planted on a hillside, thus checking dangerous erosion; about Epirus, where the peasants who needed tile to repair their guerrilla-destroyed houses figured out that they could build a road as easily as they could carry the tile on their backs from the nearest town. They built the road, and the tile was brought in by truck.

Their first information about the community-development scheme having been brought by their visitor from Patras, the Demesticans had a particular interest in discovering what the people in their neighboring town would do about it. Some went there in person over their new road, and came back to report that the major enterprise had been the production of gravel for streets and other purposes, through the reactivation of an old rock crusher that was put to work on a twenty-four-hour schedule. Instead of the sixty cents which the city had been paying, the gravel was being turned out for one and one-half cents per cubic meter. But that was only part of the work under way.

The Patrans had wanted a new sewer system, but had no adequate pipes. So they had built their sewer mains out of rock and cement, much after the techniques used by the ancient Romans, and they may last equally as long.

Frequently these projects have required the opinion of a

qualified engineer, to check the soundness of the plans. This type of aid was given as often as possible, by United Nations technicians. The engineers found that the people with whom they worked were stoutly independent, proud of their community effort, and resistant to any orders from outside. But advice from qualified sources was gratefully received. The rural Greeks are using this professional help to a degree that would hardly have been credible a few years before, when local solidarity ruled and all "outside interference" was resented.

The same spirit, the government has discovered, leads the peasants to protect and maintain the work of their own hands as they never protected facilities financed by state funds. In the days when the government used to pay shepherds to set out trees, the peasants looked the other way when goats ate the saplings, because their disappearance would mean more plantings and badly needed additional wages in the ensuing year. When the shepherds themselves decided to plant trees with the help of the CDE (Community Development Employment) funds, woe to any goat that tried to sneak a bite!

In the same spirit, the roads that the people build they keep in repair, and the drainage system they have themselves installed, they maintain scrupulously.

On the accounting side, the central government computed the total cost of labor performed voluntarily during the first eighteen months in Greece at $4,000,000, representing 6,000,000 man-days of work beginning in July 1950. Balanced against this investment, is the saving obtained in removal from the relief rolls of thousands of individuals, who were made independent of such aid through their own joint efforts.

Although the initial funds for the program came from the Marshall Plan, through the local sale of supplies imported with ECA dollars, the allocations are now a fixed part of the budget of the central Greek government. Gradually it may be possible to cancel even this support, for the rural communities themselves are steadily developing their ability to finance projects the people select.

In analyzing the effectiveness of the Community Development Employment scheme, Mr. Leet feels that it is peculiarly adaptable to rural areas, where local loyalties are easily tapped and where results are quickly visible. Old friends and neighbors have a mutual understanding, they are aware of their community's needs, and the projects they favor generate the kind of enthusiasm for a common cause which is rare in metropolitan districts.

Another valuable aspect of the CDE program is that it is government-sponsored. Any population worth its salt, Mr. Leet holds, frets at dependence upon funds from abroad, which put the people in the position of accepting foreign alms. Aid from their own governments, on the contrary, is not only their right, but their pride. When it reaches them through their own provincial officials, their sense of participation is strengthened. Home-town ties are comfortable and enduring.

A plan was afoot in an Agrinnion village in Greece, for example, to install a new water-supply project. The people realized that they could hardly go ahead without professional advice, but none was available.

One of the older men present offered a way out of this dilemma. He was sure that if he wrote to his son, a prominent Athens engineer, saying, "Son, your village needs you," the son would drop his work and come. It turned out exactly as he had expected. The water-supply project was quickly under way.

In both Greece and Korea the CDE projects brought moral and economic gains on a scope difficult to assess. Each road built by volunteer labor, and at minimum cost, had a two-way impact, because it opened markets at either end of the stretch for the inhabitants of both communities. The people who could raise more farm crops thus had outlets to a wider market, and acquired additional money to purchase what they needed. The entire area felt the stimulus.

From the records of the contracts he initiated during the six weeks he spent in Korea, Mr. Leet showed some typical figures representing projects begun in Chollo Pukdo province. There the disbursements amounted to 96,250 *hwan*, up to the date of his departure for New York. This sum had been paid out for 3,850 man-days of labor, for which the estimated increase in the income from Korean crops was about 5,675,000 *hwan*. He has no comparable notations on the Greek program, but the gain there was undoubtedly on a similar scale.

For the nations that have contributed so much to the distressed areas—and the United States is an important donor—the CDE program has particular significance. Each of these village projects helps to decrease the demands for aid from abroad, and takes that much of the burden off taxpayers all over the world.

As conditions improve in those remote communities that seem so alien to us, their national economies are being bolstered little by little. And we ourselves are coming closer, inch by inch, to acquiring these populations as future customers for our own products—instead of pouring out our sustenance in a one-way operation. And that's good.

SEVEN

WE FLY OR THEY DIE

PERU AND COLOMBIA

To AN ANDEAN INDIAN whose village perches aerielike atop some mountain crag, the plane in which he is whisked to work daily on another peak only thirty minutes away is as routine as is the 7:22 from White Plains to Manhattan, to a resident of Westchester. An automobile, on the contrary, would stop that same Indian in his tracks in fright—or incredulity. He never has seen one.

This is the transport paradox of the last twenty years in Latin America, especially along the west coast where the high Cordilleras dominate the landscape and the life of the people. Here there are only heights and depths! Roads are nonexistent in many sections. By foot or by muleback, that same half-hour hop would occupy days or weeks for a toilsome descent of one peak and an equivalent struggle upward to the next. Yet in this lofty region are located any number of villages and towns that were brought into existence by the airplane—and endure only because of them. It is of these settlements that the pilots who fly the network of local airways can say to one another with conviction,

"We fly—or they die."

If in Europe or the United States every single airliner were to be grounded through some catastrophe, the tempo of life would be slowed, but nothing drastic would happen. The air-minded would take to the railroads, the buses or private cars. Shipments would arrive later than they do, although they would continue to flow. Mails would take a day or two longer than normal, but communications would go on as usual—by telephone, telegraph or radio.

Among these Andean peaks telephone, telegraph and wireless are missing. The airplane is the only link their isolated dwellers have with the outside world. They are dependent upon it for practically everything, including sustenance. It is at once their twentieth-century pony express, and their lifeline. Its cargoes and its passengers present daily as colorful a kaleidoscope as a globe-trotter would happen upon anywhere in the world.

For example, a plane landed one day recently at Lima Tambo, the handsome airport in the Peruvian capital. Five passengers dismounted. One was a businessman as smartly tailored as though he had come direct from Bond Street. The rest were Amazonian Indians in their native garb. The plane carried a load of rubber: also some ducks and chickens. There were two goats. And three or four monkeys were carried off—whether they belonged to a passenger or were in transit as freight was not immediately clear. No one in the vicinity took the slightest notice of what was after all a routine performance.

"I can remember that at one time in Brazil, the pilots refused to fly anyone carrying snakes that were not caged," reminisced C. J. Tippett, chief regional officer in Lima for the International Civil Aviation Organization. "Occasionally one of the natives would get aboard with a boa constrictor—just a baby, not more than nine or ten feet long—taking him into town for sale to a buyer for some zoo. The pilots got to the point where they flatly refused to carry them unless they were boxed. They didn't like the idea of a boa constrictor chasing around loose in their planes."

Mr. Tippett has been associated with the development of air travel and transport in Latin America since the early flying days in the interior of Brazil, in 1940. At that time he explored by plane, at little more than treetop level, large areas until then unseen and unmapped. His group scouted the Shevanti area, discovering there a number of Indian villages no one had ever before glimpsed—or at least reported.

"As a matter of fact," he commented, "at that time the Brazilian government did not know exactly what people, if any, were in that region. It was estimated that this—I guess we could call it—new civilization, consisted of at least 10,000 men. All were fine specimens of Indians. They were tall, and painted their bodies completely red. By the way, they were also very fierce.

"The first time we flew over them they shot arrows at us. The majority of Indians would have run away and hidden themselves. These did just the opposite. They rushed out of their huts and in from their fields, and they fired everything they had at us—war clubs and rocks and stones and arrows and spears. Actually, we kept away from them. We circled the place, just out of range. Otherwise we might have caught a spear or a rock that could have fouled up the propeller or broken a gas tank.

"I believe I'm correct in saying that Brazil still has the largest unexplored territory in the world today."

It was terrain and conditions of this character that stimulated the rapid development of airlines in Latin American countries after the impetus had been given by the First World War. Colombia opened a commercial service not long after the armistice of 1918, and others followed. German interests launched a series of mainly domestic companies in Bolivia and Colombia. They flourished precisely because of the inaccessibility of many of the points to which they flew. By the time the second world conflict threatened, American authorities had become acutely conscious that this German ownership, so close to our borders, was a genuine risk, and nudged the directors of United States international capital to buy up some of the lines. This was done. A certain proportion of the investment in Latin-American air transport remains in American hands. Most of the lines are by now locally controlled, and figure prominently in plans for future development.

These plans are gigantic in scope and, at this stage, largely visionary. They are concentrated upon the *oriente*, the vast, fertile lowland plains that fan out east of the Andes—hundreds of thousands of square miles of fertile soil harboring untold wealth in minerals, timber, water power, agricultural and other resources. One day the airplane is destined to fill a significant role in opening up these wastelands, screened now by jungle and infested with all manner of insect pests, wild animals and treacherous swamps. Even when the present trackless distances have been crisscrossed by networks of roads and the wilderness begins to succumb to the teamwork of scientists and resolute pioneers, the airlines will almost certainly continue to serve this part of the hemisphere as passenger-carriers.

The headquarters of the agency are located in Montreal. Activities of ICAO, in which fifty-seven nations hold membership, range from the laying down of basic specifications, standards and practices governing practically every item relating to aviation, to the promotion of safety measures and uniform regulations for operations.

ICAO has been an affiliate of the United Nations since December of 1946. Its annual budget in 1953 was $2,817,-167. Through its staff of 425 men and women, ICAO maintains communications with ministries of aviation in dozens of lands. They keep in touch, too, with research laboratories and industrial plants, and from these nerve centers are informed promptly about the latest and best equipment for planes, for airports or for the signaling towers through which air traffic is policed.

It is the function of the ICAO Regional Office to provide to Latin-American governments, technical advice and assistance in every phase of aviation. Similar help is being given by ICAO staffers in other branches, all around the globe. The office at Lima is prepared to supply to the interested governments all kinds of information, from the construction of aircraft to methods of building instrument-landing systems, or to advise on safeguards in the drafting of aviation legislation.

This office also checks on the observance of existing statutes or international regulations regarding the safety of pilots, passengers or cargoes. It surveys aerodromes to determine whether they conform to specifications, whether proper communications facilities are available, and whether needed improvements are being made as rapidly as possible.

The personnel is prepared to plot air-traffic services; to furnish information either about the region or to it concerning the handling of craft incoming from another country, to insure efficient landings by pilots unfamiliar with the area; or to advise outgoing ones about the conditions they will encounter at their destinations. Where required, they also establish search and rescue facilities.

Their main problem has not been any lack of good will on the part of the governments to conform to all these specifications, but simply that an insufficient number of trained people are available for that purpose. Progress has been made and is easily measurable. Bolivia, which began with a line originally German, is now operating the same routes almost exclusively with Bolivian technicians, mechanics, operations officers and crews. Notwithstanding the extremely difficult conditions, this line has an excellent safety record.

To appreciate the importance of this factor in a country handicapped by transport difficulties, it is only necessary to consider the value of the main airport in the Beni section. Until recently this province had no means of getting its produce to market. Every item from abroad that was needed there had previously been brought down by river boat. It was disembarked in Brazil, then sent on several thousand miles by river steamer. Now all such freight goes by air in a fraction of the time. Even the cattle that are killed for this market are loaded into aircraft and flown to the consumer centers.

From his vantage point in Brazil, Mr. Tippett had watched the evolution of the "airplane towns" as they mushroomed up at points in the vicinity of mines—including diamond mines—that lay at high altitudes. First, an emergency landing field would be built by a crew flown in for that purpose. Then the miners would disembark, along with a few farmers. A tent colony would spring up around the landing strip, and planes would zoom in daily with food for the occupants. Then more people would arrive.

After two or three months wooden shacks would start to go up here and there, and presently small shops would be opened, catering to their trade. In an incredibly short time a complete, bustling little city would have materialized, built around that emergency landing strip.

The airline services have kept pace with the requirements of these populations so competently that roads have never become necessary. They could be built, but the expense would far outweigh the benefits. This holds true not only for Peru and Colombia, but also for Bolivia, Chile and Brazil.

Yet it is inaccurate to claim that the development of aviation is more essential in these Andean countries than anywhere else in the world. The peculiarities of Latin-American topography—along the western coast—are rivaled on the opposite side of the globe, notably in the Indonesian archipelago, in the Marshall Islands and in Samoa, by difficulties of another sort.

Here the natural barriers to easy access between communities and to the free flow of trade are not the soaring peaks of mountains and the intermittent deep valleys, but the expanses of ocean that separate island from island. Many months can be—and are—consumed in the slow rounds of the trading ships that ply the sea lanes from one to another.

Indonesia, for example, comprises some 3,000 islands, and the span from Sumatra in the west to the easternmost communities of the nation is better than 3,000 miles—as far as from London to Beirut. By steamer, at least a week would be required for the journey. By air it can be done in thirteen hours.

Civil aviation, properly developed, could speed up the momentum of progress and enormously expand both domestic and foreign markets. Alert to this potentiality, the governors of Indonesia's various states have been pressing the central government for more and better air service ever since the end of World War II. During that conflict the native population became accustomed to airplanes through the force of circumstances, as pilots of every conceivable type of Army craft buzzed into and out of their once isolated communities. Why build fleets of slow boats and ships, local officials soon demanded, when domestic aircraft can skim above the storm-tossed breakers that mean risk and delay for the water-borne?

Even while these topographical barriers are shrinking beneath the wings of airplanes that accelerate commerce and expand industry, the mountains and the seas are being spanned at an increasing tempo by radio communications that likewise make a mockery of distance. Gradually, the children in secluded valleys and on remote isles are finding themselves drawn into the radius of educational facilities that will equip them for a way of life neither their grandparents nor their parents ever experienced. It is significant of the hunger that prevails everywhere for knowledge, that the elders are listening and learning, as eagerly as the youngsters, and are humbly absorbing the rudiments of elementary schooling right down to the ABC's.

Wherever immense plains are dotted with villages, as in Asia, the airwaves pulse with programs that reach their destined audiences relatively easily. On the Latin-American continent, in the Andean region, every mountain peak interposes a separate obstacle to penetration of the radio lessons, and bounces back the broadcasts according to a principle every modern schoolboy understands. Under these conditions, fewer listeners can be reached by any one program.

That fact failed to dismay one determined priest in Colombia, whose imagination was so powerfully stirred by the example of other countries that he struggled unceasingly to find at least a partial solution. He not only found it, but has so dramatically proved its effectiveness that his system has become a pattern in his own and other lands. He is Father Joaquin Salcedo, and his name is rapidly becoming a symbol of education by radio, internationally as well as nationally.

He chose for the hub of his broadcasts the community of Sutatenza, Colombia, only a few miles from Bogotá, the capital. Sutatenza is situated in a beautiful valley from which his transmitter could reach an appreciable number of settlements. When he began, five years ago, there was not a radio receiver anywhere in the region. By September of 1953, he was beaming his programs to 300 schools, with the possibility of raising that total to 5,000 within two or three years.

It took a tremendous effort on the part of Father Salcedo to open the original, one-kilowatt station and to launch the radio school. He had scratched the necessary funds together by dint of appeals to pastors and to local officials in each of the adjacent communities, through repeated visits, month after month.

More than their contributions was required. He needed their consent to install in church steeples and in the towers of town halls, the receivers through which the programs could be piped to the loud-speakers that were to be set up in whichever home or building was to be used for the classes. Eventually he had all the co-operation he needed. Enough receivers had been installed, the loud-speakers attached, and the listening groups formed.

From the first, this was exclusively an adult-education project, keyed to the conditions of life in the vicinity and planned for the capacities of the people, almost all of whom were illiterate. In every instance, some literate man had to be found who could function as a substitute teacher, and conduct the class. This "remote-control" staffer listened to the instructions, wrote the exercise on a blackboard, and then made corrections as the students copied the lessons into their notebooks.

Rudimentary as it was, the influence of the school spread apace, and both local and national authorities were dazzled by the results. In 1952 Father Salcedo was sent to Paris to attend the sessions of the United Nations Educational, Scientific and Cultural Organization, as a delegate from Colombia. At headquarters of UNESCO there during the meeting of the General Assembly, he took part in many a conference with the agency's executives, and found them agog to hear every detail of his enterprise. They arranged for him a UNESCO fellowship to study adult education and the use of radio in this field, which took him on a tour of some months to the United States and Canada, for consultation, exploration and just plain listening to radio programs.

In Canada he discovered almost exactly what he had been groping for mentally—the Forum for Farmers. It is a program of adult education which merges practical advice on agriculture and home economics with entertainment.

With adaptations designed to meet the particular requirements of his listening audience, this is the formula that is followed today at his studio in Sutatenza. It combines with fundamental education such basic instruction as reading and writing, civics and hygiene, religion and music. A program for men is broadcast daily from six to seven in the morning, one for women from four to five in the afternoon and a third from eight to nine at night, for both.

Special stress is laid upon arithmetic, Father Salcedo says, "because we consider it very important for accounts, in business and so forth." But variety rules. Elementary geography is blended with tips on methods of improving farm crops in the valley, and women listeners jot down recipes for new soups or other dishes, in between chats about religious culture or the structure of the local government.

Since 1948, the progress made has been "simply fantastic," in the phrase of R. P. Echats, United Nations resident representative in Colombia. Government officials were so pleased that they requested help from UNESCO in improving and expanding the facilities. As a consequence, at the end of

1953, five technicians had already been scheduled to go to Sutatenza to work out a bigger and better adult-education program, and to handle the preliminary work toward channeling the broadcasts into the schools for the children.

Concurrently with its other tasks, this staff will prepare and print appropriate textbooks that are to be circulated to the present schools as well as to future centers, to replace the simple copybooks that have served until the present.

Father Salcedo has borrowed liberally from other countries, including the United States, in shaping up the varied elements of his station output. His store of records of popular music is large and representative. He uses local talent for his dramatic productions, with surprisingly good effect. There are quiz programs and newcasts, and on Sunday afternoons from three to five comes the best loved interval of all—popular music interspersed with news and comment.

The network is growing month by month. Father Salcedo's goal of 5,000 additional receivers is coming closer to reality through the combined resources of UNESCO and the Colombian government, which have promised to produce them. They will operate on batteries because the farm areas are still without electricity. Each receiver installed is equivalent to a school, which is organized around it, and each school thus opened brings more farm families closer to information and techniques that will stimulate their crops and improve their strains of cattle, thus nourishing their bodies as well as their minds.

Across on the opposite side of the world, in Pakistan, something of a counterpart to the Colombian radio network got into production late in 1953. There the government, along with all its other plans for economic and industrial development, determined to make an effort to bring elementary education to the children in isolated towns to which transport is next to impossible. With UNESCO's help, the teaching staff was assembled and the broadcasting station built. The curriculum includes reading, geography and arithmetic, with one fifteen-minute program in each beamed to the distant schools four times daily.

To supplement and expedite understanding of instruction given by radio, UNESCO long since began a study of methods of supplying visual aids to education. Production of materials of this type is already under way in volume, and its value has been recognized. Maps, charts, film strips, posters, reproductions in inexpensive form of the great masterpieces of art and similar articles, are employed in conjunction with lessons by radio. They fill in many gaps for the students in Pakistan, in Colombia and elsewhere, bridging the abysses of illiteracy and bringing millions out of that darkness and at least a few steps forward, into the realms of knowledge.

As Father Salcedo has demonstrated in Colombia and others in different lands, a little of such yeast can produce quite a powerful ferment.

EIGHT

THE CHILDREN
BEFORE BIRTH AND AFTER

PAKISTAN

EARLY IN the morning there is coolness on the wide, flat roof of the Lady Aitchison Hospital in Lahore. It makes a fine classroom, while the sun still dusts with silver the dome of the mosque across the way, and vagrant breezes stir.

So the students come there, to perch along the wide parapet that makes such a comfortable bench, until heat and glare drive them to cover. They look fresh and crisp in their white uniforms, like student nurses anywhere—a bevy of dark-haired, dark-eyed girls all wearing the long Pakistani trousers, gathered at the ankle, and straight, belted tunics. Instead of caps, they bind their heads in smooth scarves that are caught neatly at the back, and ripple across their shoulders.

They belong to a generation of pioneers, and their earnestness betrays awareness of the role. They are Pakistan's emancipated women—the first to dispense with veils and the purdah of their Moslem mothers—and they walk cautiously, partly in the shadow of traditions they have challenged.

Many thousands of their age-group in this young republic have fanned out into shops and factories and schoolrooms, to work and to teach with their faces bared to the world for the first time. But the girls on the hospital roof are the future nurses and midwives who are bringing modern ways and methods among their people in the field of childbirth and maternal care, long enmeshed in superstition and the abracadabra of self-made magicians. Less than the others, can they afford the luxury of mistakes now and then.

At the midwifery school founded in Lahore by the government of Pakistan and equipped by UNICEF, the students are not overly tense about it. They have youth on their side, and the powerful prop of science and sound education. They have not forgotten how to laugh, and sometimes they sing. Most of the time, the conditions they see about them are a bit too grim for levity. The need for their ministrations is almost incalculable.

In Pakistan the paroxysm of severance from India, in 1947, brought chaos. As trained Hindu administrators streamed out of West Bengal to live under the New Delhi government, the countermovement of throngs of Moslems erupted into the hastily established state. Facilities of every kind were disorganized, or nonexistent. In temporary quarters, using packing boxes for desks and chairs, inexperienced and badly handicapped officials buckled down to their tasks. Swamped by the multitudes of refugees, they have been unable to do more in the intervening years than to furnish them a bare subsistence, in spite of the strides that have been made toward stabilization. Huge governmental projects under way promise to integrate the displaced gradually into the national life, but that time is not yet.

In the interim, the training school at Lahore is preparing these native young women to serve expectant mothers among both the refugees and the stationary population. By sending them out into the communities to open clinics, UNICEF hopes to reach the maximum number of persons through programs of infant and maternal care, to bring them those principles of hygiene, proper feeding and home remedies that have been so dimly understood. Ultimately, the agency believes, the training offered in its midwifery and nursing courses will enable the graduates to take over the phase of life so long monopolized by the *dais*—that strange coterie of old women, usually illiterate and steeped in witchcraft—upon whom generations of women in Asian countries have depended for centuries.

As a class, the *dais* resent the younger women as upstarts and even heretics, and object bitterly to their casual attitude toward the ancient rituals. That for so many years those same rituals failed to prevent frequent deaths is attributed to Allah's will—not their fault. Even more sharply they protest the loss of fees from patients who turn to modern medical care, since it means bread taken from their own mouths.

Fortunately, a proportion of them have proved flexible, willing to learn what they can of better nursing care. In a situation where even partially trained hands are welcomed, these women have been cultivated as valuable assets.

Within this sensitive sphere, involving as it does both religious and traditional practices, UNICEF's policy has been to tread carefully, avoiding offense wherever possible. Its students have been taught to meet the *dais* with due respect, and to show appreciation for any co-operation. Instructions given them have been to interfere with none of the customs unless they pose a risk for either mother and child; and to ignore any fee paid the *dai*, even when she took no part in the actual delivery.

The two schools of midwifery are in strong contrast. The older is unconcerned with cleanliness, ventilation or sterilization of clothing or instruments. It runs to incantations, to charms hung about the room as protection against evil spirits; to use of a piece of split bamboo to sever the cord, and a mass of freshly chewed betel, bound firmly to the baby's stomach. A common practice is to rub cow dung on an infant's arm or leg, to cure a skin eruption.

A UNICEF graduate must learn to tolerate such things, within limits. The incantations and the charms do the patient no harm, and may reassure her. The split bamboo, the mess of betel and the cow-dung applications are emphatically barred, although she is urged to avoid unnecessary friction by explaining the reasons for the ban. While she knows the basis for the techniques science has dictated, she is reminded, both her patient and the *dai* are still in the dark about them. They are more apt to be co-operative if they are told what infection is, and how it is spread by some of these "cures."

The girls have been encouraged to make of themselves a bridge between the past and the present, rather than to clash with old superstitions that still exert such magnetism in the popular mind. A knife slipped under the bed during childbirth, or the crossed sticks or tiny effigy placed beneath the mother's head-rest—none of these things actually interfere with sickroom care. They can be allowed without upsetting efficiency, just as cleanliness and order can be achieved for the patient without rousing antagonism.

The younger system utilizes every resource contemporary medicine offers, to protect the mother's health and to insure a good start in life for the child. Supervision begins in prenatal days with the same attention to a patient's health, weight and diet as Western women are given. Later, postnatal routines guard the infant against the normal perils of the important first twelve months.

In the process, habits are instilled in the mothers that often improve the health of the whole family, if only through the stress put upon sanitation in the living quarters, and in the preparation of food.

Lulled by the ministrations of both schools and the absence of tension between them, numbers of expectant mothers have responded with better spirits and quicker recoveries from confinement.

Notwithstanding their struggle against conditions of abysmal poverty, this first group of trained Pakistani midwives has set a gratifying record. Statistics are sketchy and unreliable in most Asian lands, although they are being improved through United Nations Technical Assistance advisers to governments. Taken at community levels in areas where UNICEF has been at work for more than three years, however, they show decreases in infant mortality during the first year of life, as high as fifty per cent and more, compared with the previous year.

The institution that turned out these young women is an international one. Its organizer was Dr. Jean Orkney, a white-haired Scotswoman who spent more than twenty years in India, and who is still serving the UN in the teaching field—now in Geneva. Each of her staff during the first few years—specialists in public health, district nursing or midwifery—had her opposite number among the Pakistani girls in training. Late in 1953 the international team packed up and departed for Karachi and an identical new project, leaving behind them as experienced staff personnel, these erstwhile students, now carrying on under their own power. Those first enrollees have become the instructors and the department heads. They are weathering the tests as they come, proud of their ability to grapple with difficulties, and grateful that the sustaining hand of UNICEF is still behind their collective shoulders. Its help continues.

In the space of a few years, the lives of these girls have changed radically. Most of them stepped from the deepest seclusion into the profession they had chosen, propelled by the crisis that made their nation sovereign and independent—and summoned women as well as men to help when and where they could. The enrollees at the midwifery school at Lahore were straight from purdah.

Among them was Tabinda, whose story is by this time widely known, and who has become the prototype. The day she arrived at the training school she was just nineteen, and exceptionally beautiful. Until then she had worn the *burqua* (or hood) that concealed her features from all except her own family. After she had put her signature to her application, she lifted it from her head forever.

Like her nation when it acquired independence—in 1945—Tabinda had been restless for a different kind of life.

Her father is a Moslem traditionalist, her mother is not. When her father took a third bride—having already two wives and two families—her mother took her and her older sister away, determined to give them advantages purdah had denied to herself. The older sister has since been graduated as a doctor. Tabinda hopes to become a nurse.

She has been learning rapidly. As a schoolroom she and her classmates have had the entire city of Lahore, and particularly an abandoned Hindu burning *ghat*, where live fifty of the families who crowded into western Pakistan, after partition. Life is even a shade more difficult for these people than for others, for the *ghat* was the crematorium where the Hindu dead were burned. The ashes of the pyres are still there. Around them stand the mud-brick, one-room homes of the displaced persons who have found shelter, but not much else for which they can be thankful. There is too much sickness, too little employment. Food is scarce and money is scarcer. Calls from the district are frequent, for the students.

It was at the *ghat* that they came to know Alla Raki, and she them. On both sides this was fortunate. For Alla Raki is the poorest of the poor, but she is also cheerful and friendly, and a born practical nurse. When they came to the settlement to help some mother about to give birth, she hovered about, watching all the preparations.

One day she beckoned, and led them to a *stupa*, the bell-shaped chapel of a Hindu god. The patient inside was unusually young, and Alla Raki had put everything in readiness for the delivery.

Surprised and pleased, they found that the clay floor had

been swept and spread with newspapers, that equipment, though primitive, was at hand, and that Alla Raki had lighted a fire under the peepul tree in the temple courtyard, and set quantities of hot water to boil. The baby arrived presently under reasonably safe conditions. He was oiled and swabbed, wrapped in a clean cloth, and cradled at last in his mother's arms.

"Teach a man," Begum Liaquat Ali Khan once said, "and you teach one person. Teach a woman and you teach a whole family." On that premise, the Begum has based a nation-wide program of organization and training which she has sponsored for her countrywomen. She is the widow of the assassinated first Prime Minister of Pakistan, and is now representing her government in The Hague—the first woman Ambassador to be appointed (June, 1954) by any Moslem country.

When the young midwives thereafter set about giving Alla Raki as much from their own lessons as she could absorb— for she has no education and can neither read nor write— they passed on the fundamentals of their training not merely to a family, but to the general population of the *ghat*. With her deft hands, soothing voice and neighborly spirit, Alla Raki finds happiness in serving her fellow man through the nursing talent she never knew she possessed until the white uniforms of the students appeared in the compound, to show her the way. Like these students, who have the courage to be and to do what Pakistani girls have never ventured before, she is helping to usher in a new era in public health.

If only one country were affected, the maternal- and infant-welfare operations of UNICEF would be commendable but hardly portentous for humanity as a whole. But here, Pakistan serves merely as a pattern, examined in close-up, of occurrences in scores of countries. It could as well be India or Africa, Indonesia, Burma or Paraguay. Month by month the system is being extended and the total of trained midwives is growing. Each graduate looks forward to her commencement day as eagerly as though she were to be handed her sheepskin on some college campus, or "capped" as solemnly as a nurse completing her course at some metropolitan hospital.

Her badge of achievement is a different symbol, even more indispensable in her professional life. It is a skillfully designed midwives' kit provided by UNICEF—as essential as is the small black bag to a general-practitioner physician.

Lightweight but sturdy, rainproof and dustproof, it is packed with instruments of shining chromium or steel, plastic bottles and screw-top jars, rolls of sterilized cotton or adhesive tape, a clean sheet and the ubiquitous thermometer. It can be worn like a rucksack on the shoulders (convenient when fording streams or climbing steep hills), slung as a saddlebag if she uses a horse or mule to reach her patients, or carried in the hand like an overnight bag, which it often becomes.

It is at once her apothecary shop and her miniature hospital canteen. It is her certificate of competence, too. Among natives who have learned to appreciate its importance, it has a unique distinction as a means of identification. For a midwife to arrive without her kit in these distant regions would be equivalent to the entrance of a registered nurse in any Western city to take over a case, wearing street clothes instead of a proper uniform.

No wonder student midwives wait with keenest anticipation for the arrival of their treasured kits, shipped from New York across thousands of miles. Some are carried over the final lap by jeep, some on camelback, and a few on the heads of jungle porters with spears poised in their throwing hands, alert for possible attacks by wild animals on the narrow trail. No wonder despair blankets the exercises when they fail to arrive in time for the graduation day.

For years to come, there will be far more need for their kits and their services than the Pakistani trainees can begin to fill. In East Bengal alone, 42,000,000 persons are crowded into the province (equal to the population of France), and of this total at least 14,000,000 are desperately poor. Their plight has been described in various reports (and by Sam Keeny in Chapter Five), but a fieldworker signing herself only V. F. W. recently enlarged upon a particular phase, in a letter to staff associates at New York headquarters. She was conveying to the desk workers what the arrival of regular shipments of soap meant there, in terms of health.

"Here beneath lowly overhanging grass roofs of countless mat and mud huts," V. F. W. wrote, "one baby dies every ninety seconds, before it is old enough to stand upright, and one mother dies every twenty-two minutes in the first fourteen days after her baby is born. These conditions exist wherever dirt and disease stalk hand in hand, as they still do in this backwater of Pakistan—the province of East Bengal.

"About one third of the population is too poverty-stricken to afford the luxury of soap. So they resort to diverse indigenous herbs and berries as substitutes, and even use wood ashes or soapy clay dug up from their own backyards. Or— they just do without.

"To many thousands of these, the arrival of UNICEF's soap has brought a new glow into their daily lives. Nature has blessed them with an abundance of water—good, bad and indifferent water. The word 'drought' seldom enters their vocabulary. With the UNICEF soap as an essential supplement, promotion of a more hygienic sense of living is being inculcated. Soap is one UNICEF commodity that walks right up to the doors of their lowly huts, crosses the threshold and affects their daily routines.

"On arrival by ship, the fifty-pound boxes are stored in a warehouse, then wrapped with bags to reinforce the packing, and carried on the heads of coolies to the muddy banks of the river. There they are loaded on ungainly river boats, laboriously paddled upstream to the first railroad depot, piled into the box-wagons (freight cars) and sent to the district offices. The soap then moves out to the areas by meter-gauge trains or motor trucks, and is carried over the last miles to the villages by bullock carts, sampans or coolies.

"In these small towns the children especially line up for the distribution by the appointed native committees—and that is when Abdul, Shareen and all the other small *butchas* gleefully wend their ways homeward at eventide, jealously clutching the little squares of golden goodness—UNICEF's soap!"

In 1951 East Pakistan received from UNICEF 300,000 pounds of soap, which benefited 33,000 children and their mothers for almost two years. Then another 215,000 pounds were shipped, which is reaching 50,000 individuals per month. The total has just now "touched the fringe of disease prevention," the fieldworker added, and the schoolteachers are enthusiastic about the disappearance among their pupils of the itch infection called scabies, as a consequence of their cleaner bodies and garments.

She tucked into the letter some snapshots she had made of a group of children from the Tejgoan village orphanage. They were paddling happily in a slough in only their shorts, under a brilliant January sun. All were energetically sudsing, sloshing and scrubbing one another's backs, with the older youngsters supervising the ablutions of the younger ones, and UNICEF soap getting a mass workout.

Joanna Monnik, a young Dutch nurse who went there in 1949 as a member of the WHO-UNICEF malaria control team, needs no snapshots to etch East Pakistan scenes into her memory. She knows them well, and has left her own imprint on them.

On arrival in the country she was sent to travel with a team engaged in spraying a large district with DDT, against malaria. Her assignment was to demonstrate to mothers and to the local *dais* elementary techniques of safe delivery and infant care, and to conduct nutrition demonstrations, distributing rations of UNICEF dried whole milk to mothers and serving it in liquefied form to the children. En route she collected data for the malaria project, which covered 194 square miles, with a population of 250,000. Before leaving a community she would set up a child-care station and train two or three native women in its operation.

Repeatedly her full schedule would be interrupted for days

of jeeping over roadless stretches and shallow streams, in search of sites for child-care schools, and rounding up adequate utensils for mixing the milk powder.

In steamy sunshine and in chilling rain she went from village to village and hut to hut, palpating the spleens of youngsters in search for malaria symptoms; taking blood smears for analysis; and giving instruction in sign language, about atabrine pills for malaria victims, or the proper method of bathing a baby. She supervised the digging of trenches for disposal of garbage; distributed ointments and medicines; registered expectant mothers; taught elementary personal hygiene and the care of the sick, and held a weekly clinic in maternal and child care, plus two weekly classes for rural midwives. "Jam," as she is nicknamed from her initials, didn't have time for "sittin' and knittin'."

At Gouripur village in Mymensingh province she best demonstrated her perseverance and dedication, through establishment of a maternal- and child-welfare clinic. After weeks of patient cajoling of the "head man" and other local bureaucrats, carried on mainly by gestures, in the absence of an interpreter, she finally won their consent to her use of three small rooms as a dispensary. The largest was eight feet by six. Delighted with her acquisition, Jam lost no time in hitching up her skirts, rolling up her sleeves and getting down on all fours in the manner of her Dutch housewife ancestors, for a thoroughly satisfactory scrubbing of floors with old-fashioned soda and hot water.

Next she brushed white paint carefully over everything, including the underside of the shelves, until reflected sunshine chased out the gloom. Bottles, bowls and cans soon shimmered in neat array on the clean shelves. Tables and chairs were moved in and clear water drawn from the well and stored in the *jalas*. The dispensary was ready, and so was Jam. But her patients, it appeared, were not.

For three weeks, from morning until the evening shadows lengthened, Jam waited and no one came despite her stubborn progress from door to door, explaining and inviting. At length one day a distraught father rushed in with a desperately sick baby in his arms. It was all too obvious that the dispensary had been his last resort. Nurse Monnik had a case worthy of her mettle and her talents, and she won it handily. The baby was revived. Next day two more fathers straggled in with their infants.

Attendance increased slowly. Tots were brought in by fathers, older brothers, uncles and guardians, and soon Jam's enterprise was tagged by her teammates "the paternal and child clinic." Orthodox Moslem women in the district refused to enter it, even when shrouded in their *burquas*. But that is history now. Jam's skill in treating their sick babies won their hearts and their confidence bit by bit, until the place was crowded regularly with mothers, big sisters and aunts bringing toddlers to be checked over at stated intervals. Jam learned enough of the regional dialect to dispense with sign language, and chatted with them fluently. They became her devoted friends.

She passed the acid test by sticking by her post throughout summer monsoons which forced the malaria-control team to approach many villages in the native boats, and when the peak was reached in August of 1950 and the team suspended operations for a month, Jam filled in the time by organizing a midwifery class at the Mymensingh clinic.

Mrs. Grace Bok Holmes, of the UNICEF headquarters staff, who paid a visit to the post that year, spent one afternoon as a silent witness in the dispensary waiting room, while Jam treated patients in her inner office. The New Yorker carried away a graphic memory of the routine as each mother arrived with a baby, marched to the shelf along the wall, stripped the youngster and laved and rinsed him carefully, tossed out the soapy water and sat down to wait for their summons to the sanctum.

All was peaceful that day until one woman, plainly a newcomer to the dispensary, spat betel juice onto the floor. In a trice she had been pounced upon by the others, babbling reproaches. Without understanding a word, Mrs. Holmes easily deduced that this native habit was not to be tolerated within these walls. Presently, under the indignant insistence of the waiting group, the offender meekly took one of the basins and a bit of soap, got down on her knees and scrubbed away the stain. Thereupon everyone relaxed, beaming at the repentant sinner and at one another in self-conscious virtue.

The influence this one devoted nurse has had in East Pakistan is best computed through her total of more than 100 maternal- and child-welfare clinics opened and staffed during her stay there. She has since been reassigned elsewhere.

On that same tour, Mrs. Holmes sensed that something about her appearance was exciting an exaggerated curiosity among the natives. Mystified, she asked the UNICEF personnel about it. They chuckled, confirming that she was indeed a novelty. In that country of uncut tresses, she was the first woman the natives had ever seen who wore her hair in a bob. Next time she faced a group, she explained to them through an interpreter that American women often wore their hair short, because it was so cool and so easy to care for especially when traveling. Smiles and nods of agreement spread around the room, and her hair style grew less conspicuous, she felt. At least, until she decided to give herself a shampoo.

The day was hot and the sun bright, so Mrs. Holmes took a container of water and found a place under a tree, partly shaded. A group of children playing nearby gathered around her to watch. She dampened her mop thoroughly, reached for her tube of cream shampoo, pinched off a bit and lathered her hair briskly. As the suds foamed up, shrieks burst from her juvenile audience and she peered around to find them wildly pointing, jumping up and down in their agitation. Out rushed her hostess, only to laugh almost hysterically at them all. The children were screaming that the American was on fire—that smoke was bursting from her head!

In Pakistan, both East and West, UNICEF has organized four nursing and midwifery training schools. They are at Karachi and Peshawar as well as Lahore, in West Bengal province, and at Dacca in eastern Bengal.

With 22,000 more midwives, the country would have one for every 120 births per annum—a target which, without international aid, it would need 200 years to meet. In Lahore alone, in 1950, there had been only one health visitor for every 150,000 of the population, stationed in 126 centers and serving the Punjab's 19,000,000 inhabitants. The present goal is one health visitor for every 10,000, or about fifteen times the total active four years ago.

The challenges to UNICEF in Pakistan have their counterparts in the Western as well as the Eastern Hemisphere. The needs are variable, but permanent. Just after the last war the agency concentrated on salvaging the child victims of that holocaust, gathering up the orphaned and the starving, the maimed and the blinded, and feeding, clothing and sheltering them through those first chaotic years of helplessness and dependence. Out of this wide and merciful program came UNICEF's reputation for having protected some 60,000,000 boys and girls from either death or serious illness, up to 1950. The agency is currently reaching 2,000,000 children each month.

UNICEF was established on December 11, 1946, as an integral part of the United Nations, designated as "an international co-operative on behalf of children." Maurice Pate of the United States heads its executive board of twenty-six members. Its revenues have come mainly from governmental contributions, and by January of 1954 its receipts had reached a grand total of $299,337,000. By far the largest single donor—for a total of $97,231,000 up to January of 1954—has been the United States, but this country can by no means claim the highest per capita contribution. As of the latter date Australia had given $1.38, Brunei (North Borneo) $1.06, Iceland $.96, Switzerland $.60, and the United States $.56 per citizen.

Dedicated to the alleviation of malnutrition, disease and physical handicaps among underprivileged children of all lands and races, UNICEF has been since its inception the pet agency of all delegates to the United Nations and of their governments. When it makes its reports to the Economic and Social Council, of which it is a unit, even Communist representatives listen respectfully. Except for Yugoslavia, which has been a consistent and generous contributor, none of the Communist bloc has participated in UNICEF work since 1950.

Once the postwar emergency was past and the tracing services had restored most of the "separated" children to their families, close relatives or foster parents, UNICEF's value was too deeply entrenched in the public consciousness to permit its demobilization. The program shifted, but the policies survived. Hand-in-glove with the WHO, it has moved repeatedly into areas where disaster has struck, to distribute emergency rations or administer DDT or penicillin, to avert epidemics.

In Brazil it was first to reach the drought-ridden northeastern states with relief supplies in 1952, and its powdered milk helped mightily to fend off threatened starvation. In the Assam province of India, when earthquakes followed by floods racked up a tragic total of deaths, UNICEF was on the job. Late in 1953 it approved emergency allocations for children in Korea and in Japan, where floods and crop failures were spreading misery, and also sent help to the earthquake-stricken Ionian Islands of Greece. And in the Himalayan *terai* it was an important factor in clearing that jungle region of malarial mosquitoes. There UNICEF, collaborating with WHO and FAO, helped the government of India to carry through a joint project that brought down the incidence of malaria in the western district from 53.7

per cent in 1949 to nil, in 1950. In the eastern *terai*, where dusting operations began a year later, the rate of infection among babies fell from 76.7 per cent to 2.6 per cent.

The terai covers 1,500,000 acres of once productive land, lost to civilization centuries ago. Its early dwellers had constructed an immense network of irrigation canals and reservoirs to water their fields, but carried the system to such an extremity that the walls were weakened and the reservoirs collapsed. When the survivors of the resulting floods deserted the region as swamps, the jungle and the insects took over. The territory had two types of malaria mosquito, which spread the disease at different seasons of the year.

As happened in Afghanistan under similar conditions, dusting of the swamps and jungles with DDT was undertaken by combined teams of the agencies and the government. There too, the district was won back little by little, as the swarms of mosquitoes vanished and the bulldozers of the FAO rolled back the masses of undergrowth, trees and vines.

The wild elephants, tigers and other beasts retreated many months ago farther into the jungle, and of 100,000 acres newly opened to cultivation, 30,000 have been resettled. Trees have been felled and stumps uprooted, and a 10,000 acre seeding and demonstration farm was set up by the administration of the province of Uttar Pradesh. The Indian government and the International Bank helped to provide tractors and other equipment.

All around the world, not only in Asia, UNICEF carries new impacts, major and minor, to the children of the nations. If the whole cyclorama of its activities were to be capsuled into a single sentence, it might approximate the answer a small Peruvian boy gave when asked whether he knew what those initials stood for.

"Of course," he retorted. "That's the American word for milk!"

His grasp of UNICEF's international scope was clear despite his overgenerous credit to this country. His confusion was natural enough, for UNICEF bought more than 400,-000,000 pounds of milk powder during its first six years, much of it from the United States. More than half of that total came from government surplus stocks, and cost only one cent per pound. A single large purchase, in the spring of 1953, was 10,000,000 pounds of surplus skim-milk powder, also from the United States. Since then, in fact, the agency has made a routine of purchasing milk powder in those quantities.

From these sources, UNICEF has served milk to 11,500,-000 hungry and sickly youngsters for varying periods, in fifty-seven countries.

Staple as it is, the distribution of milk has been only one of UNICEF's continuing ministrations to the younger generation. It has furnished the penicillin, administered by teams supervised by WHO, that has rescued hundreds of thousands from the blight of yaws; the BCG vaccine issued to more legions, against tuberculosis; the DDT that has banished malaria for millions, at a cost in many regions of only about fifteen cents per head; and the basic drugs, the artificial limbs, the layettes, the Braille volumes and the preventive treatments for those threatened with blindness, as well as retraining for many already sightless.

163

Because domestic production cuts both costs and delivery time, UNICEF has made a policy of sponsoring erection of local plants for the manufacture of penicillin, BCG vaccine and DDT. One of the largest is under construction by the government of India, near Poona in Bombay. It will have a capacity of 750 tons of DDT annually, for the output of which UNICEF has supplied $750,000 worth of equipment and supplies.

BCG plants have sprung up at Ankara, Turkey, and Guayaquil, Ecuador. The Ecuador unit is large enough to insure protection for 500,000 children yearly throughout Latin America. It will serve, too, as a training ground for technicians from all over that part of the Western Hemisphere.

Between 1948 and 1954, UNICEF helped to provide eighteen of these local laboratories. They are in Mexico, the Philippines, India, Pakistan, Czechoslovakia, Poland, Yugoslavia, Egypt, Israel, Taiwan (Formosa), Iran, Trinidad, Thailand and Uruguay. This list alone is evidence of the recognition governments are giving increasingly to the problems of mothers and babies, whether in Pakistan or in Paraguay. From the latter country, after a 12,000 mile trip by jeep and plane in Latin America in 1952, Dickson Hartwell, of UNICEF's Public Information staff, sent the following description of UNICEF work there.

"To discover what health facilities were like here until recently, I drove out a few miles from the capital (Asunción) of self-respecting but poverty-ridden and war-devastated Paraguay. I visited a 'health center' which provides virtually the only medical care for an area of 5,000 persons, mostly farmers trying to entice a living from an un-co-operative land.

"The locked, weathered doors of the place seemed not to have been opened in months. In the overgrown backyard where a goat munched peacefully, I met the 'director.' He wore a dirty white suit, two days' growth of beard and tennis shoes with laces split, and had a weaving, bleary-eyed appearance which suggested periodic and recent indulgence in a potent brew. He had been trained as a pharmacist, I learned, and operated this health clinic three mornings a week, assisted by a 'nurse' who is paid the equivalent of $1 per month. To this man, mothers trustfully bring ailing children.

"The clinic, in a community called Capiata, is one of dozens which were operating on such a basis two years ago when Drs. David Hunter and Manuel Salcedo of UNICEF came to Asunción as investigators. It was one of a chain built by the government to serve people living along the country's only main highway. Hunter and Salcedo found sound buildings, and nothing else. Some of the centers weren't operating at all."

The government, Mr. Hartwell reported, approved plans proposed by the survey team, including an offer of equipment from UNICEF for an adequate system of health clinics under government supervision. His account of the results continues:

"I saw the effects of this co-operation in the first center to be rehabilitated, which opened in April of 1952. Here in the small (5,000) community of Fernando de la Kora, is a functioning health center that any city in the United States twice its size would be proud to acknowledge.

"The clinical work—advising on health problems of mothers and children—is in the hands of young and competent physicians. The clinic functions daily. Its equipment, from sterilizers to examination table, is the most efficient obtainable. Already 700 mothers and children are registered on its rolls. When hospitalization is needed, a UNICEF ambulance takes the patient to Asunción.

"In this center an expectant mother who otherwise would give birth to her baby without trained help, on the bare floor of a mud hut, can learn to prepare a layette that costs as little as ninety cents. (The crib is homemade, but sturdy.) Diapers are made from cloth purchased by the government in huge quantities and sold at cost. The expectant mother does her own sewing, having learned it in the prenatal Mother's Club, which gives seven lectures weekly on such subjects as nutrition, or control of infant diarrhea. Each lecture is followed by an appropriate movie.

"This is her first contact with scientific health principles. After her baby is born, she joins another of the center's clubs. Here she is taught the fundamentals of homemaking, not as they are practiced in the United States, but as she can practice them in Paraguay. Among a primitive people whose main guidance has been only superstition and instinct, this is a tremendous advance."

By the end of 1953, ten such centers were active in Paraguay. Parallel developments are under way in a number of countries of Central and South America. Their significance is tellingly conveyed by Mr. Hartwell's anecdote from Brazil, which he also visited during his jaunt by jeep.

"There aren't many statistics available in Brazil to prove how valuable UNICEF's work here has been," he said. "Statistics often are not kept. When I asked a German priest in the village of Pacotí for the figure about the drop in infant mortality due to UNICEF, he pointed toward the bell in the church steeple.

" 'It used to toll the death of a baby three or four times a week,' the priest said. 'Now it rings but three or four times a month'."

NEW TOOLS CUT CLEAN

AFGHANISTAN

THROUGH THE ages, until the catastrophe of World War II rocked civilization and its tremors were felt even in the far places, Afghanistan had been one of the parts of the world where time was static. All that has changed. Although with many a skip-beat, it is moving again and the tempo grows steadily more regular, less erratic.

Well before the conflict ended, the twentieth century had come clamoring for admission to this time-locked territory, still Biblical in its pace, its customs and its costumes. In the capital city of Kabul, perched on twin mountains beyond the Khyber and the Lataband Passes, life has taken on something of a roller-coaster character as two widely separated eras— past and present—merge dramatically. In this strange period of transition, electric streetlights dim the beams of candles, and camels contend for right of way with motor trucks. The patina of dead centuries peeps through fresh paint, but the people, in general, approve. And why not?

All that is inherent in its extremes of heat and cold, mountain and desert, bless and burden this land. Here is a country of probably 12,000,000 persons (two thirds of them women and children), rich in natural resources but poverty-stricken as to housing, public health, food and fuel. Here is a population recurrently subject to epidemics of typhus and malaria, largely unaware of the rudimentary elements of sanitation or medication. In the entire nation there are only 100 physicians, and but one of these a woman. Since purdah prevails and the veiled women will rarely consult a male doctor, it is understandable that in some sections, of 1,000 live babies born, 400 die during the first few years.

Yet qualified agronomists assert that Afghanistan's latent potentialities, if cultivated, could insure its people a comparatively easy existence. The sour, neglected soil could be sweetened and coaxed to produce far more abundantly; mineral deposits could be exploited, and education could develop the natural talents of the population.

Geologists incline to the theory that the terrain harbors oil in plenty, at least for domestic consumption. Six potential oil basins have been identified. Plans were in preparation for drilling, to confirm these indications, until the government of the USSR protested the presence of foreign oil experts, so close to its own borders. Thereupon the work halted. Two formidable barriers in any case confront the explorers —lack of funds to sink experimental wells, and of pipe lines to bring the flow out of the desert.

Survey teams have reported that Afghanistan sheep could probably produce the finest Persian lamb pelts on the world market. But demand for them has been dipping in recent years as drought, epidemics and food scarcities have slashed both the quality and the quantity offered for export.

Various foreign experts, at first depressed by the scant

living Afghani farmers obtain from their fields through their antiquated methods, have been cheered by the discovery that a resolute government is driving forward on several fronts with a corrective program replete with promise. Upheaval for the population and its traditions is implicit in these plans, so it is well that the people, like Barkis, "are willin'." To those most intimately concerned, it is the goal that matters, not the break with the past.

The resurgence began with a request from the Afghan government to the United Nations for a study on a national scale. Recommendations were asked for as to where and how treasury funds might be channeled with greatest effectiveness, to improve the economy. The survey was made in 1949 by the Food and Agriculture Organization, and the findings submitted simultaneously to officials at Kabul, and to FAO headquarters in Rome. Initial contracts were signed for those projects on which mutual agreement was reached that they could be most easily activated, and within a few months international teams had been recruited and were in the field there.

Other specialized agencies were promptly drawn in, but the key job remains that of the FAO. For it is agriculture that causes the nation's severest headaches, as well as its finest ultimate prospect of a better life. The difficulties are enormous, but diminished ever and anon by the response among the people, whose receptiveness and co-operation are outstanding.

In spite of almost staggering frustrations, a factor that has kept United Nations men plugging away at the job has been the sparkle that lights the eyes of an average farmer or sheepherder at the demonstration of a new tool or a better method which promises increased production or a slightly higher income. Now and then reaction has been so instant that a thoroughly weary expert has shed fatigue on the spot, and has practically walked on air, back to his jeep. Each day has its challenge for the technicians in Afghanistan, and boredom grips them only when they cannot be constantly on the move and in action.

The nature of the country has made transportation their enduring obstacle, and it is far from solved. A jeep is their usual vehicle. Trucks loaned by government agencies are available sporadically. When both are lacking and business calls, FAO men mount a proffered camel or a burro, gnashing their teeth meanwhile at the deliberate pace of their steeds. On occasion such transport can be an advantage, however. For ninety per cent of the Afghans are agriculturists and perforce nomads, roaming widely in their search for pasturage for their flocks.

Tribes move en masse. Tents and rugs, baskets and bundles are strapped to the humps of camels, and babies thickly swaddled are cradled peacefully atop the lot. All lighter possessions are loaded onto the asses, who go plodding ahead with pots and pans jingling, a few odd chickens with their legs snugly tethered squawking a protest, and bundles of fagots bobbing at every step. Where grass is found they pitch tent and remain, cultivating what land they can until their animals have nibbled the surrounding acreage down to the nub. Then the whole process must be repeated.

Trains do not exist and the sparse, rough roads chew viciously at vehicle tires, jolting the passengers unmercifully.

Camels and donkeys wisely abandon them for the smoother surfaces of roadside paths. Under such conditions education especially has suffered. Schools are few and teachers scarce. Medical care is unpredictable, and victims of accidents had better choose to be injured at minimum distances from towns, in case they are going to need any form of hospital care.

Where no roots have been put down over so long a period, farmers have had neither the opportunity nor the incentive to develop sound methods of soil cultivation. Agriculture was overdue for an elemental revolution that is now in process.

Of this dawning era, the scythe has become the symbol.

Until it was brought to them by an FAO mission led by Dr. Willi Sommerauer, a young Swiss, the only farming implement in general use had been the sickle—straight-edged and set at right angles to a wooden handle. It was a cheaply made, fragile and unreliable tool, given to frequent breakage, after which it was tossed away. Their harvesting routine, Dr. Sommerauer had observed, differed little from those of their earliest ancestors. Seated on the ground, the farmer grasped a handful of grain with one hand and swung his sickle with the other, then shunted himself along to widen his cutting arc by no more than the length of his arm at any one movement.

Under the sponsorship of the government, the first move made was a demonstration of more efficient hand tools, including the hoe and the rake. The young Swiss staged it neatly. He had with him three Austrian peasants in their native dress, all skilled in use of the scythe. In a fascinated circle the Afghani crowded around, intent and puzzled, as the Austrians went to work with long, rhythmic strokes. In clean and regular swaths, the ripe grain fell. The spectators were astonished. The scythe-wielders scored a "smash hit."

From tribe to tribe these demonstrators worked their way, stimulating wonder and, for the most part, enthusiasm for the innovation. Occasionally plans went awry and only a handful of tribesmen turned out to watch the Austrians work. Of one such episode Dr. Sommerauer wrote that "the demonstration at Kunduz left much to be desired. At first only a few farmers were in the field. Then the local commandant hired 30 tambours, one piper and one clown, which cleared the bazaar and brought the crowd to the field. But this is not the type of demonstration that will have a lasting effect."

To insure the best possible use of the tools he was introducing, Dr. Sommerauer devised a plan. He asked the district governments to invite only the ablest farmers. At the close of each demonstration these men were encouraged to try their own hands at the scythes. An assistant unobtrusively graded them on their performances, as "very good," "good," "mediocre" or "bad." Then the farmers were called together, the basis of distribution was explained to them, and the best of the scythes were awarded to the mowers whose names topped the list. Hoes, rakes and hay forks were also awarded. The system won general approval.

Each scythe conferred on a man incapable of using or maintaining it, the FAO realized, would prove a hindrance to the agricultural program instead of the intended help. Wherever tools were issued, rechecks were also important, and it was often necessary to give further instructions.

The FAO men and the government estimate that this training and equipment has increased the productivity of individual farmers nearly fivefold. In this country of limited rainfall, lacking both large-scale irrigation schemes and modern farming equipment, larger crops in any single harvest will have clearly visible effect on the meals consumed by any family. There will be more bread, more fruit and more vegetables to be set out on the straw mats the Afghani use instead of tables. And the cattle, too, will get their share of the increased yields from arable lands.

With the droughts of past years to sharpen their memories of hunger and of short rations for man and beast, the Afghani farmers with rare exceptions are welcoming the new tools wherever they have been introduced.

The scythe as a natural evolution conforming to their pattern of life, has carried them forward at least fifty years in their agricultural practices. What the tractor, the reaper and the binder did for Western farmers within living memory, the scythe has done for the farmers of Afghanistan within the last few years. More complicated mechanical contrivances would only have baffled the majority. They have taken to the simpler equipment, on the contrary, with gusto.

"Of course," one returned fieldworker commented with a grimace, "we can't always be certain they are going to be used in orthodox fashion. I remember one demonstration where some members of a particularly warlike hill tribe showed up and eyed the disassembled scythes covetously. When a couple of them snatched up scythe blades and swished them around their heads with the zest of men who had just struck pay dirt, they obviously had plans for adapting them in ways that wouldn't have promoted agriculture in Afghanistan. Things like that have to be watched pretty carefully."

Fortunately, such disconcerting incidents have been rare. Among the more pacifically disposed plainsmen, a greater obstacle than misdirected enthusiasm has been the disinterest that cropped up at intervals. Sometimes groups who wandered away from the demonstrations said frankly that they preferred the sickles they had always used. Others were simply disinclined to work any harder or faster.

Dr. Sommerauer and his assistants, who tabulated attendance, found the balance running strongly in favor of adoption of the scythes. At Imam Saiyad, the record showed that "the farmers watched with great interest and at the close, the acting chief of the village read a memorandum to the effect that they woud like to purchase 500 (scythes)." And in Ghazni, where the governor and the local commandant were among the 300 present and soldiers were stationed around the field to lend dignity to the occasion, the farmers to whom scythes were offered "went straight away on their own initiative back to the field of wheat and finished cutting it."

The most exhilarating experience the young Swiss had, however, came on his visit to a national exhibition during Jashen (independence) celebration in August of 1952. To demonstrate how sugar is produced, the largest company had arranged a display of cultivating and harvesting implements, which caught his eye because several appeared to be of domestic manufacture. Examining them more closely, Dr. Sommerauer discovered that they were surprisingly well-made reproductions of the hand tools his group had been introducing throughout the country.

"Even a scythe had been copied," he reported, "but with less success than with the digging and pulling hoes, or the beet-thinner."

For the young man who had labored tediously to develop some appreciation of these tools, that chance encounter must have generated pride and hope. The brief mention he made of it in his report was factual enough—rhapsodies by fieldworkers would spread consternation at headquarters. It is a fair guess, however, that a mental flashback brought him memories of the reapers he had first met squatting in their fields and inching their way along, gathering their crops with patient inefficiency, and also that he left the exhibit with a new spring in his heels and the assurance in his heart that those long hours under a hot sun had not been wasted, after all.

Using another hand tool unfamiliar to the Afghani, it was no trick at all for a second FAO technician to point the way to an overnight increase in the country's yield of salt. This man had visited the open salt beds and had watched the painfully slow, laborious method of scraping the surfaces of the deposits. One day he showed up with several hand saws. In a trice he had proved to the crew that it was far easier and much quicker to separate a number of foot-square cubes of the soft mineral by just sawing them out. Shoveling was unnecessary—the blocks could be piled one upon another for transport.

"There wasn't a bit of sales resistance," he reported to his teammates as they gathered for their evening meal.

By the end of that first day's work, the crew had had the salt moving at a rate that taxed their transport system. Joy reigned at the salt flats, except among the patient burros on whose backs the cubes were slung for the first stage of shipment, and who seemed a bit offended at being so often roused from their siestas, to jog away with another load.

A number of European plows, suited to the pulling power of a team of oxen, have also been demonstrated in Afghanistan. Formerly a fringe of stubble and weed remained after the first furrows had been set with the native wooden types, and two crossplowings had been necessary. With their wider, deeper blades, the new ones turn a greater quantity of soil, and cut substantially the time once required to ready a field in the traditional fashion.

These departures from the old ways have already begun to make a difference in domestic production, and each development is followed with keen interest by the population, in the hope and belief that more and better food will result. Afghani authorities, however, are looking beyond mere subsistence, toward real prosperity. Hence their keenest attention is focused on the contributions veterinary science is making to the karakul sheep industry, which is of paramount importance to the nation's finances.

For years karakul sheepskins have been the country's top export item. More than 1,000,000 persons are employed in the industry. In 1934, when a monopoly was started, the herds were in flourishing condition, and 1,100,000 pelts were being sent abroad. By 1945 the volume had risen to 3,200,-

000. The following year it dropped to 1,700,000, and continued to decline as drought lingered and epidemics spread. When the first FAO men arrived in 1950, the sheepherders were desperate.

The experts assigned recognized at once the necessity of making an extensive analysis of basic conditions. It was begun promptly by Dr. D. A. McPherson, an authority on animal diseases who had been sent to Afghanistan by the agency. Exhaustive laboratory work was indicated. Dr. McPherson was directed to the huge, modern slaughterhouse at Kabul, where he was given carte blanche by the director, a government appointee. He found at hand a wealth of material.

With hundreds of carcasses of freshly killed sheep and cattle available for examination, Dr. McPherson was quickly able to identify three or four prevalent diseases—pox, worms and some animal tuberculosis—in addition to the rinderpest he had expected. He stopped speculating about the slump in the sheepskin exports. The reasons were abundantly clear.

From Kabul the team took to the field to try to locate the sources of these infections, and to inspect the conditions under which the sheep were maintained. The job took weeks and entailed thousands of miles of travel over areas passable only by jeep. But the expedition was productive. They visited numerous tribes, examined their flocks and their pasturage, listed the multiplicity of ticks and other parasites that were infecting animals through their skins, and peered into water holes, in which they found a profusion of disease-bearing snails.

They watched, too, the commingling of healthy animals,

newly arrived, with others that had drunk for some time from these insanitary pools, and could judge fairly accurately where many of the danger points were to be mapped.

Back again in Kabul, they laid the findings before administration officials. Their list of suggestions for curbing and abolishing the pestilences was specific but, at least for the government men, fairly stupendous in scope. Ticks and other pests on the sheep could be destroyed by DDT sprayings. Serum injections could protect the healthy animals and cure the sick ones. Far more difficult to achieve would be the winter feeding, the reseeded ranges and the adequate supplies of clean water the team was advocating.

Only a modest beginning has been made as yet on these long-range objectives. Scientific surveys have begun—as the team proposed—to locate underground streams that might be tapped for additional drinking facilities. If they succeed, the flocks can remain stationary on pastures normally abandoned while the grass is still plentiful, but where the water has given out. Another idea was that quantities of hay might be stored on the range at stated points for winter feedings, rather than driving the sheep to lower grounds, with consequent loss of weight for the animals, and some of the herders have tried it out.

The most far-reaching and expensive investment of all— as well as one of the most essential—called for a systematic program of improvement in the types of grass sowed for pasture. The need is country-wide, and the probability is slim that the plan can be adopted within the immediate future. The same holds true for the experts' recommendation that measures be taken to clear the snails out of the water holes. These pests are seasonal and must be attacked in all districts simultaneously during a given interval, four times each year. Up to now this has not been possible.

Word had spread among the sheepherders, mysteriously—as it does even in remote hinterlands—that some foreigners had arrived to help them. From far and near, they came swarming to plead for advice, as the veterinarians began their survey, late in 1950.

At one isolated post, just before the advance team was due to start back to Kabul, the visitors asked that a call be sent out for 80 sheep owners to come in the next day for a conference about their flocks. Next morning, to their astonishment, they found themselves encircled by more than 200 men, begging with tears in their eyes that the team stay with them. Under the circumstances, all that the UN men could do was to pledge their word to return as soon as possible with necessary equipment, and to save as many sheep as they could.

They kept that promise. They have gone back to the area more than once, and conducted there vaccination and inoculation campaigns against sheep pox and other diseases. And they have met repeatedly with the herders to discuss the ailments of their animals and to explain the control regulations that can prevent extension of infections.

Another and different impetus toward improvement of the Afghanistan sheep is making good progress. This is the selective-breeding project conducted by J. E. LeRiche, an FAO authority with an international background. Mr. LeRiche's first impression on meeting the Afghan breeders was of their pride in their special lore, handed down through generations, from father to son. These men wear their distinctive, fezlike karakul caps as badges of honor. They know their strains thoroughly, and can accurately predict the color and conformation of sheep that will result from given matings between the two types—the blacks and the grays. When the discussion veered to betterment in the quality of the pelts, however, he sensed that he had something of value to offer them. Up to that point he had begun to wonder about it.

They paid relatively little attention to segregation of their finer rams for breeding purposes, Mr. LeRiche learned. When he touched on the possibility of producing in this way sheep with more lustrous coats and tighter, longer curls—especially valuable for the export market— conversation languished and a perceptible coolness developed.

Luckily he had brought with him from Southwest Africa a series of photographs showing the stages of identical experiments conducted by sheepbreeders there, and the successive generations of finer and better animals that resulted. He opened his brief case and spread the pictures before them.

This was competition his audience was bound to respect, for no prouder label is brandished on the fur marts today than that of Southwest African Persian lamb, and its rise to pre-eminence has come only within the last several years. His exhibit was scrutinized with rapt attention. The mercury inched steadily upward as the group conceded that the FAO man had made some telling points.

Selection of the best potential breeder-rams got under way very soon, according to principles outlined by Mr.

LeRiche. The finest are gradually being culled and studied, particularly as to the luster and the length of their hair. From such ancestors there may yet come a new and superior type of Afghanistan karakul sheep, for whose silky pelts women will clamor, and which can be fashioned into coats of surpassing quality and style.

Success in the venture should mean a gratifying upcurve of export earnings to be funneled back into other income-producing industries. This in turn would be reflected in a rise in the average wage and living standard of Afghanistan families.

While Dr. McPherson and Mr. LeRiche busied themselves about the production of better sheep, E. P. Pattison, another member of the FAO mission, embroiled himself unexpectedly with veterinarian problems. Pattison is a sugar-beet specialist, commissioned to advise the Afghan government on ways of expanding and improving the output of sugar from the beets cultivated in certain areas. His excursion into the livestock field was hardly premeditated.

He had gone to the town of Baghlan in northern Afghanistan, to study the beet plantings in the vicinity of a large, modern mill. To this mill the beet crop from miles around was brought to be weighed and pressed into sugar. Huge mounds of the discarded beet pulp had accumulated on the bank of the Kunduz River, near the building, and Pattison had been thoroughly taken aback when he was informed that for the fourteen years the plant had been in operation this residue had been routinely tossed into the water to be carried downstream.

Horrified at the wholesale waste of a product he knew to

be filled with vitamins and so highly prized as fodder in the United States that farmers pay as high as $95 per ton for it, the FAO representative inquired why it had not been fed to the starving cattle he saw everywhere, and whose plight he had been pitying.

He was suddenly up against a stone wall of prejudice. Afghan farmers were convinced that sugar-beet pulp would poison their animals. As insurance against any cow or sheep taking even an accidental nibble, they had insisted that it be thrown into the river. They had fed it to their herds years before, and quite a number had died.

Protests and arguments proved futile. The natives rejected all his pleas that they at least experiment, because beet pulp alone was bad for the animals, but that they thrived on it when it was properly mixed with other ingredients. The Afghani retorted that this American was crazy. Balked momentarily, Pattison turned his persuasive powers on the mill owners. If the pulp could be proved safe for the stock, he argued, they would have much to gain and nothing to lose. Eventually he won his point. The owners advanced funds to purchase fifty head of cattle and sheep, all of them skin-and-bone and considered already doomed.

On a plot in the mill yard within view of the carts and camels arriving with beets to be weighed, the FAO man set up a corral, installed his "victims," and concocted his formula. It was a ration of thirty-two pounds of beet pulp, two pounds of molasses, two pounds of cottonseed cake and six pounds of wheat straw. This he began feeding to his menagerie. Then he sat back to watch the natives watch the animals they confidently predicted would be dead within thirty days.

Except for the wheat straw, his mixture employed products that had been almost entirely useless to the country. Some of the molasses from the sugar beets had been utilized to briquette coal dust from a local mine, of which the total output in 1950 had been 5,000 tons. The cottonseed cake had been used as fertilizer or to fire the boiler, kindling being at such a premium that any wooden structure, temporary or permanent, risks disappearance stick by stick into the home fires of passing natives.

Such were the components of the mash he served regularly to his hungry boarders, under the suspicious eyes of the drivers of the carts, and of the neighboring farmers. Instead of succumbing, the cattle got fatter and friskier—day by day.

Less than a week after the experiment began, Pattison one morning found more than seventy animals in his pen. Since there had been no natural increases, he was puzzled.

A few days later he counted nearly 200 crowding the corral—and light broke. He grinned. Under cover of darkness, the farmers had begun slipping their own beasts under the wire for a free feed!

Then came an urgent telegram summoning Pattison back to Kabul. No replacement was immediately possible. Studying his dilemma, he began to perspire a bit. Without a technician at hand to keep watch on the situation, the risk was considerable that rinderpest might break out in that herd, and that the experiment would boomerang. One dying cow in that enclosure, and the blame would unquestionably be placed on the feeding. But he had to leave.

In the capital his superiors, alerted by Pattison to the situation and its dangerous implications, likewise held their heads and hoped for a break. Reassurance came some days later in the form of a message from Dr. McPherson, Pattison's relief. Dispatched promptly upon his arrival in Baghlan, it carried good news.

"Pattison's feeding operation highly successful," it read. "Phenomenal gains all livestock. Farmers demand exceeds supply. Sufficient pulp stored for present operations."

The head-count in the corral at the end of the suspenseful thirty days, Dr. McPherson wrote, was 400, in place of the original fifty. They included twenty horses, ten buffalo, twenty calves and "some donkeys." Pattison had taken the precaution of ear-tagging each of his initial group with a number and the weight of the animal before the special feeding program was started. It was hardly necessary to check these records. A casual glance into the pen was enough to silence even the doubting Thomases.

Nobody was happier about it all than the mill owners who financed the test. As for the riverbank, it has long since been plucked clean of the wispiest remnants of beet pulp.

On one of his infrequent trips to FAO headquarters in Rome later, Mr. Pattison added a postscript to the story. He had also fed the beet mash to some camels, although "at great risk to life and limb," since the camel drivers still believe it is lethal for their own beasts, and express their resentment vehemently.

"I found the camels almost too receptive to my ministrations," he laughed, "but considering the fact that there are 2,000 camels delivering beets there every day in that factory yard, the temptation was just too much for me."

Ordinarily this expert spent his time surveying sugar-beet fields and indicating to government representatives a number of ways in which the output of sugar for the population might be expanded. He emphasized that the hills were too crowded to allow the maximum growth for each beet; that plantings by drill rather than by hand will yield four times as heavily; that the system of irrigation was erratic, causing shrinkage in some spots and spoilage in others; and that the beets needed more regular hoeings, to encourage development.

The soil and climate, on the other hand, were well suited to this crop. If the necessary changes could be made, construction of additional pulping mills would be more than justified, and the entire industry could be enlarged.

Except for his gamble on the feeding program at Baghlan, Mr. Pattison left to his qualified teammates the complicated job of dealing with veterinary problems. They have had marked success at it, mainly against the rinderpest epidemic that afflicts cattle generally throughout Asia.

Against this plague FAO men use the now standard inoculation with a vaccine that was first cultivated in the albumen of eggs. But in Afghanistan, not only is transport drastically restricted by the absence of roads, but the refrigeration necessary to retain the potency of the vaccine is almost unknown. Some variation of the accepted routine had to be found. Ingenuity provided one.

"Walking laboratories" were introduced. These are teams of goats, taken along by the vaccinating squads. At some predetermined point on the march the goats are inoculated.

When the resulting fever has reached the indicated height, the goats are killed and the vaccine is made on the spot from their spleens. It is then carried in a thermos packed with snow from the mountains, until the waiting herds are reached. Vaccinations must be made quickly at the rendezvous, otherwise the injections will lose their effectiveness.

New teams of goats must be picked up along the trail, inoculated, killed at the right moment, and a fresh quantity of vaccine made ready before the squads reach the designated meeting place with the next herd.

By expedients of this kind, tremendous progress has been made against the epidemics in Afghanistan since the first FAO men arrived there in November of 1950. At that time a serious outbreak was under way in Herat province. It was their initial challenge. They began wholesale vaccinations at once, explaining through government interpreters as they worked, precisely what they were doing and what reactions would be observed in the cattle treated. Native helpers were assigned to observe each step and to learn the techniques. As they gained experience, these men were sent to adjoining districts, as vaccinators and as teachers of still other groups.

By March of 1951 more than 30,000 head of cattle had been vaccinated and the epidemic had been arrested. The campaign was then carried on into the north. During April and May another 30,000 were treated, and by the end of 1951 the total was 1,000,000 head protected. The cattle owners have taken over the cause with enthusiasm. They have been rigid in establishing and maintaining controls over movements of herds, understanding as they now do, that the infiltration of animals carrying rinderpest brings the disease among healthy ones.

Sometimes an individual technician in the field chafes at what he considers the too deliberate tempo of his own section of the national program. FAO executives who review all reports and evaluate the whole picture know that the advances are steady and that the pace will accelerate.

One project that has already gone into higher gear, in fact, is that administered by the lone Japanese technician in the field in Afghanistan. He is Kinston T. Keh, who began more than a year ago to introduce proper methods of growing silkworms, as a cottage craft. It was intended to provide employment for large numbers of women and older men who spent their days almost entirely in idleness, and for whom fieldwork was too arduous.

Mr. Keh's explorations uncovered ideal conditions for his specialty. Around Kabul and Kataghan, his reports showed, the dry atmosphere and the mild spring and autumn seasons were well adapted for the growth of the silkworms.

In the area, too, the soil is exceptionally rich and deep, suitable for mulberry trees. And although there is full employment, the farmers greatly needed a side line to bolster their earnings. By early 1954, they had found one—through Mr. Keh's activities.

He had imported from Japan stipulated types of cocoons, and slips of mulberry trees appropriate for Afghanistan, after months of surveys and of instruction to the natives in the care and handling of the worms. Much of the land he chose for his mulberry orchards had been scorned as "bad land," which no one else wanted to cultivate. Those acreages are paying dividends now.

At Pul-i-Khumri, where a huge new cotton mill had been opened and the government, with FAO co-operation, was cultivating a larger and finer cotton crop, families of workers had been installed in a big housing development near the mill. To this colony went Mr. Keh, tape measure in hand. He studied the floor space and arrangement of the rooms, checked the length and width of typical ones carefully, and inquired about the placing of sleeping mats in the bedrooms. The insallation of frames for silkworm-breeding would not interfere unduly with the living habits of the inmates, he found, nor with normal traffic through the rooms. Housewives, grandparents or children could tend the silkworm beds and make their spare hours profitable through their earnings, while the men labored in the fields.

From his knowledge of the market and his experience with the Afghani, Mr. Keh was convinced that it would be comparatively easy for the population in the Pul-i-Khumri to realize approximately $1,000,000 (U.S.) between 1953 and 1957, if he could enroll them in his program. He felt that conditions were so favorable that second and third crops of silkworms each year should not be difficult to produce.

His report to Rome headquarters in January of 1954 announced that the demand for silkworms was tenfold higher than he was able to fill, and that the new industry was still picking up momentum.

Mr. Keh had once mentioned proudly, in a report to headquarters, that "the British Ambassador came to see me and my (silk)worms." But the peak moment of his mission arrived in January of 1953, when he was given an audience with the ruler, Mohammed Zahir Shah, at the royal palace in Badachur Park. When he was presented by the Governor-General of Katakhan, Mr. Keh opened a small cardboard box he had been clutching tenderly as he hurried through the streets of Pul-i-Kuhmri, and offered the sovereign "the first autumn cocoons ever raised in your country."

The king's comment to this United Nations expert was a striking testimonial to the value of his work. He expressed the hope that the Japanese technician might extend his activities "all over the northern provinces as far as Badakh-Shan, where my people of Cavakhana, who have been prohibited by the State—with a great deal of difficulty—from cultivating opium, are now in want."

"I often think," the king added, "that an agricultural industry such as silk production could help their means of livelihood, as it is a product which, because of its value, can support expensive transport costs, and can be exported under difficult conditions. I will give an order for your journey to be made easy, when you go there."

In the national perspective, however, the silkworm enterprise is dwarfed by the implications of the cotton crop, which could make Afghanistan self-sufficient in domestic production. Attainment of that goal would mean a saving of many millions of dollars of foreign exchange—just as in Ethiopia—since the yearly imports of cotton textiles would be unnecessary.

W. W. Dickinson, cotton expert with the FAO mission, is the man behind this plan. His operations have begun to show exciting promise. He has participated not only in development of the mill, but also in the cotton fields. There he directed far-reaching changes in treatment of the soil, and experiments with healthier types of seeds, to determine which of them offer the best return in the form of fat white bolls. Progress has been steady. The newer, younger plants are lifting their heads proudly above those of their straggling, rather anemic predecessors.

Directors of the cotton company have given him ready co-operation, even when it led them into unfamiliar paths. When, for example, he proposed that the public bazaars be used for showings of a series of documentary films on cotton-growing, to spread understanding of the regional scheme, they were nonplused. Only about twenty per cent of the people had ever seen films of any kind. But the executives went into conference—and came out smiling. They told him to "go right ahead."

He went, from village to village, over a circuit previously chosen. The showings were local sensations bordering at times on a stampede. The bazaar throngs elbowed and jockeyed for position, following the disclosures about the life and death of a cotton plant as breathlessly as though it had been an absorbing drama. Within a few weeks he had exhibited the reels to 3,000 farmers and had even arranged exclusive showings for women. (Being in purdah, they could not otherwise have attended.)

Another pet program of the cotton specialist was a tractor-driving school, to which young Afghani were admitted only after careful selection, including medical tests. The tractors, owned by the cotton firm, employed steam power because fuel for diesels is scarce there. The Dickinson reports about the recruits were emphatically optimistic.

"The Afghani whom I have had the pleasure of training,"

he wrote, "are proving very adept and are learning fast. When we first started I did not believe that they could progress as rapidly as they have. It seems that all a person has to do is to show an Afghan the way, and you have a hard time keeping him from going too fast. By the time I leave Kunduz these men will be qualified to run both the International Harvester 'M' and the Ford 'Ferguson.' All the drivers will be qualified to handle a two-furrow plow and a disk-harrow.

"One man is able now to run a 'middle-buster.' It took two weeks before he could run a passably straight row. Today it is perfect."

All of the operations described above are typical projects of the FAO, but taken together, represent only a segment of the global activities of that agency. Field programs are directed from the Rome headquarters. The staff is headed by Dr. Philip V. Cardon of the United States, and totals more than 1,000 men and women. Seventy-one nations hold membership in the FAO, and many have provided highly qualified techicians for its missions. Yet its share of the TAA budget amounted to only $5,000,000, in 1953.

In Afghanistan as well as in other countries, FAO has worked closely with the WHO, due to the prevalence there of malaria. This disease, as much as any factor, brought about the deterioration of the national economy over the centuries. Together, the international teams faced the task of treating hundreds of thousands of villagers and tribesmen, and the reclamation of an entire region that had lain fallow for 800 years.

The story goes back to the days of Genghis Khan and his marauding hordes. Before the arrival of the "great destroyer" the Afghani enjoyed, under one of their most progressive rulers, the benefits of a vast network of irrigation canals and reservoirs that had turned the Kundus—between the Hindu Kush range and the Oxus River—into a fertile valley. But the conqueror was careful to leave nothing so important intact. After smashing the dams and insuring the draining of the canals, Genghis Khan and his men left the devastated territory to be monopolized by millions of malaria mosquitoes. The jungle crept over the newly made swamps, and the population retreated farther and farther from what came to be known as an abode of death.

"If you choose to die, go to Kundus," runs an old Afghan saying.

Repeated attempts to reclaim the land failed. The colonists were either killed by malaria or fled. Then in 1950 the WHO arrived.

Its gigantic task went forward doggedly. Quantities of DDT arrived and the job of spraying the jungle growth began. Trained squads of men in the green uniforms of the malaria-control detachments were sent out, to dust every individual who could be reached in villages on the fringes of the Kundus, as they had earlier dusted residents of Kabul, Kandahar and other cities. Even the tribesmen who passed that way were halted, and they and their families and animals underwent the dustings.

The effort was successful almost to the point of embarrassment. Within two years the mosquitoes had vanished and the jungle was gradually being pushed back by the bulldozers and tanks of the FAO teams. Then a popular cry arose for DDT dusting of the entire Afghanistan population. The campaign developed pressures that rapidly became uncomfortable for the WHO. The preventive measures it had employed had smothered in the incipient stages the usual annual epidemic of typhus, and the Afghani were avid to have this ancient enemy stamped out once and for all. They wanted DDT for everyone, and they wanted it right away!

Neither the supplies then in the country, nor the trained personnel would have been adequate for a program of such dimensions, and it was physically impossible to handle. The limitations had to be clarified for the people, and assurances given that the goal would be reached eventually. As the facts penetrated, the drive lost its intensity, and the UN men breathed more easily as they took up their routine once more.

On the 500,000 acres of cleared land, rich with the loam of ages, the FAO participated in establishing the cotton-growing belt, and in recruiting workers for the big mill. This plant produces the cottonseed cake mentioned earlier in the present chapter. The by-product has been adopted as winter food for the karakul sheep and is contributing toward a decrease in the deathrate among the flocks—once as high as forty per cent.

Meanwhile throughout Afghanistan, WHO staff workers have teamed as usual with a UNICEF mission, in medical and health programs for mothers and babies. UNICEF has been backed to the hilt in its Afghan work, by a government alert to the critical need for maternal and child care. Clinics set up to train girls as midwives have been well patronized by the shy Afghani women, from their opening day.

Then in 1952, this program got an unexpected accolade.

Two daughters of Prime Minister Mahmoud Khan Ghazi enrolled for training in the midwifery school that had just been dedicated at Kabul.

The gesture was revolutionary. Among elite families in Afghanistan, the custom of isolating women in purdah had been resented by many girls for a long time, without result. Here at last were two high-born young ladies who dared to cast aside their veils and to offer their strength and their services to their countrywomen. Prejudice against participation by women in any kind of community activity is traditional and deeply rooted. Now it had been openly defied, and in the tents of the nomads and behind latticed windows in the towns, the whispering of women rose like the rustling of leaves in the forest.

It is too early to judge whether such cultural changes in this picturesque land will keep pace with economic shifts, or develop at a more deliberate rate. UNICEF workers represent practically the only outside contacts Afghani women have had. The daughters of the prime minister have finished their courses. Further evolution of maternal and infant care will depend upon them and upon their fellow students who are taking it over gradually. This part of the future is theirs to mold.

The coming years are far more promising than the past. There is, for example, a plan drawn and ready for execution as quickly as it can be financed, that will one day produce the country's first airport. The site—in the southwest area—has been selected, and a number of international airlines have bid for permission to use its facilities. It will, they say, cut flying time from Europe to the Far East, by five and one-half hours. At last travelers can enter and leave Afghanistan quickly and easily, skipping the hazards and the hardships of the Khyber and the Lataband Passes, and a secluded nation will find itself next-door neighbor to the world.

Sentimentalists may weep for the passing of the charm they find in the "unspoiled" existence there. The Afghani have relatively few regrets. They find too much of compensating excitement and promise in the minor miracles of modern medicine, agriculture and technology, opening up to them vistas of emancipation from drudgery, cold, illness and—above all—hunger.

TEN

THE HUNGRY, HAPPY HAITIANS

FROM THE air as the plane spirals in for a landing at Port-au-Prince, Haiti looms ahead like a great, horseshoe-shaped emerald on the broad bosom of the Caribbean. At closer quarters as the craft noses down toward the airfield, the panorama tends to lose some of its allure. Bleak expanses of denuded slopes and hillsides become visible. Gullies like deep gashes in the landscape are mute evidence of erosion far advanced, and clutters of native villages comprising mud huts propped up with poles indicate flaws in the mammoth jewel. Yet vacationers who debark in a flutter of expectation, eagerly on the trail of the exotic and the picturesque, will not go away disappointed. Haiti (meaning "land of mountains") specializes in contrasts.

It boasts vivid tropical flowers to screen the harshness of its primitive rural homes, and strikingly modern buildings to dazzle strangers, along its city streets. It is a country in flux, sponsoring a vast national-development program on a long-term basis, which has within the last few years wrought significant changes in the lives of its population. Sight-seeing charabancs bowl through this summertime Switzerland, pausing alongside some of the symbols of the new era, and the alert mind registers an impression that the present is beginning to draw ahead of the past. But the future promise can be estimated only against the yardstick of things as they used to be.

An average visitor will wince at the obvious drastic poverty of many of these happy-go-lucky, leisurely people, while storing up mentally quite a different kind of travelogue for home consumption. Why should a stranger bother about substandard living conditions, when the Haitians themselves look so carefree? One glimpse of a *coumbite*—that traditional feature of Haitian agriculture—and the fleeting traveler is charmed, and convinced. Life in this island is all play!

So it seems. Deeply rooted in the mores of the people, the *coumbite* operates effectively to get work done in the fields, on the docks and elsewhere, along the same psychological principles applied by businessmen who pipe music into their factories to stimulate the rhythm and the tempo of production. Among the races of African descent, it has a far older history. They have always capered as they work, to the obbligato of their own primitive instruments.

Watch what happens at a wharf in Haiti when there is a ship to be loaded with coffee from a warehouse nearby. The *coumbite*, a co-operative group of laborers, moves in on the job—barefooted, white-shirted, with trousers rolled to the knees. Equipped with long bamboo horns and beating time on shells or bones, the men heave sacks of coffee beans to one shoulder and go prancing en masse down and across the gangplank, to deposit their burdens in the hold. Then they go dancing and jigging back for another load, until the warehouse is empty and the ship is full.

In rural areas when a peasant has land to be cleared or prepared for planting, the *coumbite* goes at it collectively, much as house-raising or corn-husking bees are conducted in other countries. Work progresses to the sound of drums and songs, and is invariably followed by a feast at the expense of the landowner. The Haitian is a gregarious individual. He extracts a great deal of social satisfaction out of his *coumbite*, and is far less productive when grubbing along alone without its stimulus.

Outsiders well may question the efficiency of the system, which is so popular that it attracts far more participants than needed, until they are tripping over one another and retarding rather than helping in the task. It has not promoted the reputation of the Haitian worker, since excessive numbers demand employment on any given contract. Too many ultimately share in the total compensation, and strict observance of minimum-wage regulations (3.5 gourds or about seventy cents per day) is defeated.

In the *coumbite*, however, lies the germ of the cooperative institutions that Haiti is likely to develop in the future. Basically, it has much to contribute.

The spirit rather than the social significance of this spectacle impresses the onlooker. It is as distinctively Haitian as the palm trees, the musical Creole patois of the people, the quaintness of their plastered, thatched-roof dwellings or the swaying grace of their women en route to market, balancing wide baskets piled with produce atop their heads. (Except for ox carts or the saddlebags of the burros, this is the usual means of portage, even for heavy loads.)

For a long time to come, the picture is not apt to change radically. Haiti has too far to go and its people too much to overcome, including their own disinclination to alter their accustomed ways, to justify hope of any metamorphosis. And their understanding and initiative are imperative if the broad, intelligent plans bueprinted by their government are to be realized. The surge of enthusiasm is still to come.

With increasing frequency, however, dapplings of comprehension and appreciation flash up to delight and encourage the Haitian fieldworkers as well as the international teams active in the joint effort to stabilize this republic on an even economic keel.

One of the emissaries who can talk with elation about progress is Vinton L. Burns, a youthful, congenial Jamaican who has been for more than two years in the island as an FAO adviser on forestry problems. Of the devastation wrought upon Haitian agriculture by almost total deforestation, Mr. Burns has a clear perspective. He speaks Creole fluently and is devoted in his reconstruction activities. His success with the people, however, is traceable to a personal quality. Once he launches into discussion of the struggle to recarpet these mountains and valleys with the velvety green of pines or mahogany trees, his genuine liking for the Haitians glows through all he has to say. It is hardly surprising that their responses have been warm, even if gradual.

Vinton Burns especially likes to recall Dominique, who became a crusader in the cause of reforestation. Public recognition has been much too slow of the fact that the slashing away of the valuable hard woods is at the root of the landslides and the eroded fields, and the Jamaican has been unremitting in spreading his gospel of forest protection and replanting.

"One day," he relates, "I was driving through a country section with the minister of forests. We came upon a hillside where there was quite a stand of cedar, and there we saw a skinny little fellow, Dominique, felling some of the trees. I stopped the jeep and called to him in Creole, 'Look here. You are breaking the law.'

"So quickly that I realized he knew he might be called to account, he dropped his tools and came running over to us. 'Oh no—I'm not,' he retorted. And he fished up from his pocket a permit to cut the trees. It was duly signed by the local forester.

"One look assured me that it was genuine. So I turned to the minister and said in English—which Dominique does not understand—'You see what we are up against. This man can't be stopped from cutting down these trees, nor can he be prosecuted. I shall simply have to go back to the forester and explain to him all over again what is involved. If these trees had been permitted to grow for another five years, they would have brought fifteen dollars each. If they had grown for fifteen years, they would have been worth seventy-five dollars. As it is, they will only be turned into charcoal, erosion will set in and the soil will collapse off this hillside, and everybody will lose, all around.'

"All the while, Dominique stood looking earnestly from me to the minister and back again, as though wondering what all the fuss was about. I climbed into the jeep again without any further word to him, and we drove away.

"Two months later I was bowling along in my jeep in the same neighborhood, when Dominique came tearing out to intercept me, shouting excitedly, 'Mr. Burns! Mr. Burns! Stop! Come—I have something to show you.' Curious, I halted the jeep and went with him. He led me around to the back of his place and pointed. Imagine my astonishment to find that he had there a whole patch of ground, neatly planted with cedar seedlings—a healthy little nursery.

" 'Why—this is wonderful! But how did you know what to do?' I asked him. 'I didn't explain anything to you!' Dominique radiated pride. 'I guessed it!' he said. 'You seemed so serious when you were talking with the minister, I knew it must be important. So I figured it out that this was what you would want.' "

Dominique's ardor has not flagged. He is a big man now in his community, for he has appointed himself patron saint and protector of all trees, large and small. After a thorough coaching by Burns as to the necessity for replantings and the results that can be expected, he went to work to enlist all his neighbors in the cause. As many seedlings as could be absorbed were obtained by Burns through the Haiti forestry department and consigned to Dominique, who has distributed them to his band of volunteers. Every available vacant space in the area now has its miniature nursery, and a sturdy little forest of cedars is emerging in precisely the vicinity where Dominique not many months ago was undertaking to hew away the only remaining trees.

Thousands more such penitents as these must be enrolled, and years must still pass before the pines and cedars will gain a foothold again on the hilltops where they used to spread protectively above the flourishing coffee shrubs. Meanwhile the campaign to win the people to support the drive goes forward by means of varied types of educational programs and demonstrations.

When President Paul Magloire proclaimed the nation's first Arbor Day—in May of 1953—Vinton Burns cut short his home leave, and flew back to participate in the momentous event.

Although these islanders have been slow to grasp what forestry development can mean for them, they have been quick to avail themselves of another type of project, the most encompassing of its kind anywhere in the world. This is the campaign launched by the World Health Organization to stamp out yaws—a blighting, disfiguring disease that has tormented mankind for centuries. It flourishes chiefly in hot, damp climates in hinterland regions where neither medical help nor such cleansing agents as soaps are readily at hand.

In Burma, India, Thailand, Pakistan and elsewhere, yaws is being attacked on an increasingly wide front. Numerically, the programs in these other countries are far larger. In Haiti, however, for the first time the drive is total and national. No element of the population has been missed in the attempt to ferret out all who have been infected by, or exposed to yaws. The international teams have been and are roving the back roads, checking, inspecting, treating all who can come—either afoot under their own motive power, or carried pickaback by relatives if they are already disabled. Many have crawled miles to the clinics, on all fours, to get treatments.

The implications for Haiti are important, for yaws has not only spread misery wherever it has touched, but it has also been for many generations a constant drag on the economy, decimating the producers among the population in the hinterland. In urban centers, or wherever people habitually go shod, yaws is virtually unknown. The infection flourishes, instead, among barefoot natives who apparently contract it in swampy areas.

The disease is not a killer. It is seldom fatal. But it warps and corrodes both flesh and bone, attacking babies as well as adults. Beginning with painful skin eruptions akin to boils, it spreads gradually along the surface of the body, boring in at last to the bones, which it leaves permanently distorted in the same way as arthritis. Although caused by a spirochete almost identical to that of syphilis, yaws is not a venereal disease. It is transmitted by contact, and especially and ironically, through the kisses affectionate mothers or older sisters so often bestow upon infants.

In the continuing struggle to conquer yaws and to reduce it to an insignificant, controllable fraction, modern science has put into the hands of the clinicians a tiny but powerful dagger with which to slay this dragon—the hypodermic needle filled with penicillin. One quick stab and it's over, in the majority of cases. The painful eruptions begin to subside overnight. In milder cases, they disappear within a few days. Even in those of long standing, healing has been usual within a few weeks, and only a minority of advanced patients seem to require more than two injections. Twisted bones remain. They are due to disappear in future years, as the boon of penicillin is carried to all parts of the globe where this natural enemy continues to survive, and victims can be treated in the early stages.

It took only a minimum of urging to bring the Haitians into the health centers in search of this panacea, as the news percolated up the mountains and down the valleys about the rapidity and permanence of cures through penicillin. For they had had earlier experience with more prolonged treatments that proved considerably less effective.

By the time the WHO began its work against yaws in the island—with the Children's Fund as usual supplying the stocks of penicillin—the Haitian government was keenly alert to both its humanitarian and economic facets, and was prepared to co-operate to the full. At hand were statistics left by the American Sanitary Mission, which had battled yaws in Haiti from 1944 through 1946, treating annually in that period, 205,000, 183,000 and 244,000. The Haitian public-health authorities had carried on as best they could up to 1948, through eleven clinics, six of them operating full time. Intramuscular injections of bismuth preparations used in those days, however, proved even less potent than intravenous ones of arsenicals, administered earlier by qualified physicians. Yaws had again become rampant. The American Mission had reported that eighty-five per cent of the rural population was affected. After 1948, the proportion was uncertain.

One of the deterrents to success in treatments with arsenicals was the fact that they required repeated visits by patients ,and that the Haitians were lax about coming to the clinic more than once. Therefore the speedy recoveries

after only one injection of penicillin were almost provi-
dential. From the personal testimony of Arthur Wakefield,
some of the cures were nothing less than spectacular.

Mr. Wakefield had visited some of the clinics during the
two years he spent in the island as chief of the United Nations technical-assistance missions. "It's practically un-
believable," he declared as he paused at headquarters in
New York, en route to a similar mission in Burma. "One
morning I went to a tiny clinic well up in the mountains.
That day I saw there a boy of about ten, who had been unable to stand for the last few years, because the soles of his
feet were covered with the sores. This youngster crawled
along the ground like a serpent, hitching himself along on
his little backside, and digging in with his elbows. He was
given a single injection of penicillin. One week later I saw
that same child—walking normally.

"There was a laborer there too, that morning, a man of
thirty-two. He had been unemployed for three years, the
palms of both hands being so cracked and swollen that he
could not hold any tool. He also got a single injection of
penicillin. Ten days later I saw him swinging a scythe in a
field nearby, once again earning his own living."

To Mr. Wakefield, the most remarkable fact was that
although in earlier stages the per capita cost of treatment
with penicillin has been as high as $2.25—and still is in some
regions due to transport costs over long distances—in Haiti
the rate of a single shot has been reduced to about fifteen
cents, American!

For the sum total of thirty cents, therefore, Haiti trans-
formed two helpless cripples (real or potential candidates for

relief funds) into a present and a future able-bodied work-man. Each is again capable of producing for his country, instead of being a drag upon its resources. Out of scores, if not hundreds of thousands, who can say how tiny a fraction of the whole they represent?

Calculations of the original United Nations technical-assistance survey mission to Haiti had been that over a three-year period, total costs of the country-wide campaign against yaws would approximate $2,500,000 (U.S.). This amount would cover the purchase of fourteen vehicles, salaries of twelve physicians, sixty medical aides and other personnel, 600,000 treatments of penicillin, gasoline, travel expense and similar items. The government approved these estimates in the confidence that the return to its working population of legions of yaws victims would more than justify the invest-ment.

By January of 1954, the World Health Organization reported 100,000 Haitians restored to the working force. Economists recognize how much a group of this size can contribute in raising the national production annually.

An indirect benefit of the successful yaws drive has been that the people turn readily to the clinics for treatment of other diseases affecting their capacity to work. One of these is malaria, which is gradually being reduced through DDT sprayings and supplementary measures. Another is tuber-culosis, from which a sizable proportion of Haitians suffer. The treatment in this field is both longer and more expensive than that for yaws. Therefore X-ray tests and demonstrations of proper handling of tubercular patients are conducted concurrently.

Programs designed to improve nutrition and to lift standards of living generally are taught concurrently with those stressing the need for segregation of open cases, and the diet of milk, eggs and other foods the tubercular should have.

Malnourishment is basic among the physical deficiencies of populations in underdeveloped areas, and in Haiti investigation had shown that the native meals were deplorably poor in proteins. Sea food, existing in abundance in the ocean waters that wash Haitian shores, could provide the missing element in profusion. But Haitians have never evinced any particular love of the sea, nor have they developed a fishing fleet of any importance. To persuade them to go after the fish would have meant a long period of indoctrination and training. Speedier results were imperative. So the fish are being brought to them, according to routines developed in ancient days in China, and still practiced there. This is "fish farming."

Western lands began to learn about the benefits of this form of fish culture only in the last few years. Technicians from the Orient, recruited through the United Nations or the United States Point Four program or the British Colombo plan, brought it up as a practical answer to the problem of insuring a larger and better-balanced food supply in critically needy territories. It proved to be another revelation of the advantages inherent in the global sharing of skills.

In this case a Chinese, S. Y. Lin, was chosen by the FAO to introduce the pattern in Haiti, where it has fitted with complete naturalness into the character of the country.

Mountains form eighty per cent of its terrain, and the island abounds with lakes, rivers and canals in which to breed the food fish imported by Mr. Lin—since Haiti has no indigenous fish appropriate for his purposes. In order of importance, the types selected had to be tempting to eat, capable of rapid reproduction and simple to care for. He chose carp, tilapia and sepat siam.

All three multiply with astonishing speed, make a succulent dish when prepared in a variety of ways, require a minimum of attention, and are unfinicky as to appetite. They live as happily in brackish as in fresh water. They can and will make productive, mangrove swamps that are now hopeless for agriculture. Dumped into rice fields, they thrive along with the crops, and are readily harvested with seines to increase the owners' income as well as their family food supplies. Above all, they are cheap and plentiful, once the initial problems of development of proper hatcheries have been overcome.

In Haiti—as in Thailand, where it was fairly recently introduced and has evolved into a national asset—the small tilapia has been the star of the show. It is the tastiest of the imports, and the rate of its development leaves the new fish farmers almost breathless. The fingerlings increase to a weight of half a pound in four months' time and begin to reproduce at that age, hatching new batches of from 400 to 600 young at intervals of two or three months. A single pair of the fish will, in the space of twelve months, produce approximately 10,000 by actual count.

The tilapia are mouth breeders. The father fish carries the fertilized roe pouch-fashion in his jaw, drifting them out of his mouth to become fingerlings. They hunt their food among small aquatic plants and animals, take kindly to household garbage tossed into the water, and at one year heft about a pound apiece. Whether dried, canned or eaten fresh, they make an excellent meal.

Both the more familiar carp and the sepat siam (habitat, Malaya) are also prolific. They need only casual attention, and are capable of adding to Haiti's food supply both variety, and the quantities of protein it has been desperately needing.

With a small, homemade pond into which he can slip the breeders, a Haitian farmer can with little or no trouble maintain close to his own house an almost inexhaustible natural larder. He need only dip his net, to assure his wife and children a nutritious meal at trifling cost, and he is showing every disposition to make such procedures a habit.

When he arrived in the island in the autumn of 1950, Mr. Lin's first move was to confer with government administrators about the building of experimental hatcheries, according to plans drawn up before the contract was signed with the FAO. Work on the construction of the first ponds, at Damien, began in November of that year. By October of 1952, twenty-one ponds had been completed at Damien and at Mariani, the largest measuring 2,700 square meters.

In February of 1951 the first of the new fish arrived from the United States—carp fingerlings from Alabama. Tilapia obtained from Jamaica were brought in in July of that year, and by the end of December had multiplied to thousands. Twenty-three of the sepat siam were shipped from Singapore to New York and flown into Haiti in August of 1952. From

experiments at the government hatcheries, Mr. Lin estimated that a yield of 1,000 to 2,000 kilograms (a kilogram
equals 2.2046 pounds) could be expected annually from each
hectare (2.471 acres). His computations excluded catches
to be anticipated from the canals, the rivers and the lakes,
the swamps or the brooks into which these three varieties
have now been introduced in numbers.

Before he left Haiti in November of 1952 for his present
home in the United States, Mr. Lin reported extensive and
active interest in fish culture on the part of government
executives. Beginning with President Magloire, they spent
hours at the nursery at Damien, surveying the installation
and asking numerous questions about the possibilities of
extending the system throughout the country.

Owners of sugar-cane and banana plantations, alert to
opportunities to supplement the diet of their laborers with
cheap and plentiful protein food, also came to see what was
going on and to find out how to proceed with the ponds
they were considering for their individual holdings. They
lost little time in adapting the knowledge they acquired. The
Dauphin plantation at Fort Liberté had by late October of
1952 finished construction of four ponds for the propaga-
tion of carp and tilapia; had stocked a thirty-five hectare
lake on its property with the same fish, and had under consideration a plan to turn forty hectares of low-lying land into
fish ponds.

In the great Artibonite Valley development project in
central Haiti, where the government has under way a vast
irrigation and hydroelectric program in co-operation with the
United States Point Four plan, the administration of

ODVA—similar to the Tennessee Valley Authority—has made preparations to include fish farming in its development, and to build breeding ponds on a large scale. Several thousand hectares of saline lands and mangrove swamps will be turned into ponds if the plan materializes.

Since Mr. Lin's departure the pace of progress has been maintained. His successor is Shimon Tal of Israel. In addition to supervising the government hatcheries and continuing the search for favorable pond locations, Mr. Tal has concentrated on popularizing the fish as an integral part of the native diet. It has not been too difficult.

He suggested among other things, that large basins be installed in the windows of foodshops, so that passers-by might see the live carp and tilapia swimming about, and become habituated to their purchase. Information about the fish and the best methods of preparing them have been disseminated through the government's extension services. The stream of individual farmers now pouring into Damien and Mariani in search of advice about preparing their own ponds suggests that Mr. Tal is getting maximum circulation for his story.

In February of 1953 he reported cheerily to headquarters of the FAO in Rome that he had had a request from President Magloire to build immediately "a one-hectare fish pond for his excellency, on his land."

The following month Mr. Tal's summary of the situation reflected quiet gratification between its lines. March, he wrote, "should be considered as the most successful month so far in the extension activities of the project." The pond on the presidential farm at Sarthe was under construction.

Two others had been completed on the private properties of governmental leaders, and ten smaller ones were in prospect for April.

"For the first time," he added, "a supply of ten kilograms of carp from the Damien nursery was given this month to the cafeteria of Madame Magloire's Foundation. It is reported that the guests who came to the cafeteria to eat appreciated the carp very much and the manager has demanded a constant supply—a minimum of fifty kilograms a week—if we can do so."

Marketing of the fish in volume began in April 1953, with regular shipments from the Damien nursery to the Saint Marc Grocery at Port-au-Prince. Mr. Tal supervised the construction of a canvas tank in which the wrigglers could be transported alive for exhibit in a window aquarium, as well as in a concrete tank about three feet by four, and four inches deep, especially built to receive them.

For a country like Haiti, so energetically trying to pull itself up by its bootstraps on a dozen planes simultaneously, it would be difficult to find a more satisfactory investment than the fish-farming program. The appropriation approved for the initial years of construction, experiment and extension under government auspices amounted to only about $12,000 (U.S.) annually. Compared with the relatively minor expense of maintenance of the ponds, generous dividends will accrue for years to come to the Haitians who make use of this filling and nourishing staple. For more and better balanced food means greater strength for work in fields and industries, as well as heightened resistance to diseases that prey upon the underfed.

The East, then, as well as the West has had its share in bringing new skills to Haiti. The ultimate fillip in connection with the program, however, is peculiarly Oriental in aspect.

As a technician, Mr. Lin could and did emphasize the practical phases of fish culture, and the need for training of Haitian personnel to insure its continuation until it had become fixed in the island's way of life. A by-product, he pointed out, would be its contribution to the control of mosquitoes and other parasites that are eaten by the fish. But as a Chinese, he felt that there were other, cultural values, not immediately perceptible to the novice.

He urged Haiti to take advantage of its many new ponds, to introduce beautiful and exotic types of fish that would add interest and diversion. Why should there not be scenic fish ponds, stocked with commercial varieties, in parks, gardens and private grounds? In the Artibonite Valley, the authority has assured him, several such points will be provided. Moreover, as the Artibonite project nears completion, beautiful tropical fish are to be introduced into the rivers and lakes in that valley.

Even then the resourceful Mr. Lin had not exhausted his ideas: construction of fish ponds and hatcheries in prison yards, mental hospitals and work camps, he pointed out, would not only provide cheap and good food for sick people, but they also offered possibilities for therapeutic and educational purposes. They were handy, too, as reservoirs in case of fire.

Just in case the Haitians overlooked it, he added, the infant industry was bound to open up a new market for labor.

ELEVEN

TABOOS

It happens once on an average, even in sophisticated gatherings. Two smokers bend to accept a light from a third. As he waves the match toward his own cigarette it is hastily puffed out, amid soprano squeals of dismay or quick masculine exclamations.

"Three on a match—very bad luck!", caution the superstitious.

Most of the time nobody laughs. It is an accepted behavior pattern, like walking around instead of under a ladder, or dodging out of the path of a black cat that saunters across the sidewalk.

These lingering manifestations of the grip of the occult on even highly literate populations have a hundred forms. They tend to be regional in character, and what is solemnly esteemed in one area, is apt to be ridiculed as comic in others. In advanced countries the sum total of superstitions is negligible, in a medical sense. In the underdeveloped ones, they constitute a real and definite barrier to the introduction of modern health and sanitation principles. Contemporary techniques even in the raising of desperately needed crops, are subject to rejection for reasons deeply rooted in dread of the supernatural. Rigid social distinctions and cults, even among isolated tribes in the African jungles, have also thwarted minor advances.

Among the international teams struggling to raise living standards and to improve economic conditions, the utmost diplomacy is imperative, in reconciling primitive beliefs and customs with the varied activities that are designed to bring about a better life. Agricultural missions have often found themselves stymied by local philosophies or taboos, and have rapidly discovered that fierce resentments can be aroused by any tendency to ignore them. The World Health Organization representatives, however, have borne the brunt of the frustrations and have exercised the greatest ingenuity in meeting this challenge.

Literally thousands of fetishes and fears booby-trap their paths. Scores of times they have had to stand by helplessly while epidemics took root and spread, because they dared not antagonize the people they wished to aid, by violating their multifold religious or tribal convictions.

How this chasm is ultimately to be bridged remains a puzzle. The best that has been accomplished represents only a compromise, and the outlook is not too promising.

The problem is enormous, and is acknowledged as such. Yet the atmosphere is not wholly gloomy. One of the bright spots is at Lucknow, India, where an able Dutch technician, F. G. Hoek, has more than justified his quiet, persistent argument against a particular application of the caste system. Mr. Hoek is a specialist in the treatment and preparation of hides.

He was sobered but not dismayed, when he realized the obstacles to be overcome if the industry was to be placed on a sound basis in the district. The Hindu reverence for animals of all kinds carries with it a prohibition against slaughtering. The flayers (skinners) comprised only men from the lowest caste, who were not only unskilled and inferiority-ridden, but were compelled to go about collecting and carting away animals that had died of starvation. The skins they brought in for treatment were awkwardly handled and frequently damaged through gashes trained men would have avoided.

Weeks of earnest conferences with officials brought rather remarkable results. Mr. Hoek's plan of "concentration camps" for surplus animals was adopted. They are now herded off the streets and into a specified field where the hides can be taken promptly after they have succumbed, and the carcasses disposed of in organized fashion. And in a series of demonstrations to men of various castes, Mr. Hoek has convinced Lucknow residents that flaying is a job demanding skill, and that it should be open to anyone who can master its fine points. The social standing of the flayers has risen, their output has become far more valuable, and the volume of usable leather resulting has won the Dutch expert both praise and gratitude.

In Bombay, WHO workers faced and overcame a similar situation. A large herd of buffalo had been stabled in a congested area of the city, posing a threat to health as well as a nuisance, as they wandered unchecked through the streets.

The population politely gave the animals place and willingly endured the inconvenience and the woeful lack of sanitation. The dung heaps in their midst, the swarms of insects and the risk of infection were cheerfully disregarded. If sickness resulted, then the individuals must have earned their ill luck by some unconfessed offense. The buffalo could not be blamed.

Wisely accepting this attitude, the WHO team adapted it as the basis of their strategy. Appeals were made to the local officials to dignify the buffalo and protect them more effectively by arranging a pastoral area for them at the city outskirts, where they could be assured of the finest of care. The approach was tactful in the extreme—and it got results.

Today the buffalo are segregated in a gardenlike setting in Aarey, outside Bombay, abloom with flowers and lush pasturage, on wide acreage where they can munch contentedly by day and retire to comfortable stables by night. Street conditions in the city are noticeably better. Meanwhile the buffalo are producing quantities of extraordinarily rich milk, which is carefully pasteurized, thinned down with cow's milk, and transported daily to Bombay. Children who for so long lacked this benefit are thriving, in consequence. To the population, it is as novel as it is gratifying to receive regular deliveries of milk—in bottles—processed through their own modern dairy plant, instead of having it dipped from vessels of dubious cleanliness and carried home in any kind of uncovered receptacle. No municipality in India yet rivals the Bombay record in this respect, and everyone is charmed.

The success of the Bombay plan suggested to progressive Indian officials that it might be extended to other communities, and the possibilities are being explored. Some of the taboos can certainly be circumvented through the identical device of utilizing a local custom to work out a logical and practical solution.

In Ceylon, a different type of religious prejudice exists which Dr. John A. Bryant, American member of an FAO mission, found harder to overcome. Here the Buddhist religion prohibits the eating of anything regarded as having life. The ban, Dr. Bryant found, extended to eggs, of which there was a reasonably good supply. The orthodox Buddhist, he discovered, will not break open or eat an egg because the act is considered to destroy life. This rule prevailed despite the malnutrition evident among the people.

In the hope that Ceylonese who needed this food might accept it if he could convince them that eating infertile eggs would not infringe their religious tenets, Dr. Bryant carried out a "pilot experiment." He selected a dozen such eggs and set them under a broody hen, calling the attention of the boy in charge to the fact that they would not hatch and might therefore have been safely eaten. He got in reply only negative shakes of the head from the boy, who nevertheless watched attentively day after day, to see what happened to the setting.

Twenty-five days later there was no sign of a chick from the dozen eggs, and Dr. Bryant called S——— to witness.

"There, you see," he pointed out. "Those vegetable eggs will not hatch, and you would not have been taking life if you had broken them open and eaten them."

In a letter to FAO headquarters in Rome, Dr. Bryant reported later on his effort.

"S—— usually brings me about seven or eight eggs every day," he wrote, "but recently, despite the change to cooler weather, higher local egg production and even higher egg prices, I have gotten fewer eggs from him. Perhaps he is convinced. Time will tell."

In various regions of Asia the ban against destroying life in any form has even precluded the taking of preventive measures against insects or vermin carrying disease. Sometimes objections were raised against the use of DDT to eliminate the malaria mosquito, or the flies that threatened a populace with typhoid.

In other cases oddly humorous protests were encountered. A farmer in Iran, for example, complained that DDT sprayings of the houses to rid them of mosquitoes, bedbugs and flies interfered with the cultivation of crops because he and his friends were no longer awakened from their siestas by these pests. They had lost their "alarm clocks," and could no longer get in their usual stint of labor in the fields, before sunset!

On occasion, under these circumstances, medical teams found it helpful to characterize germs as poison. This made sense to the native populations, and circumvented the necessity of determining whether the germs had true life, or not.

In Buddhist societies, where the prohibition against taking life is dominant, the international teams have won cooperation in ridding communities of infection-carrying insects whenever they have been able to persuade someone in authority to assume the responsibility. Other groups have steadfastly refused to permit any campaign to free them from plague-infested rats. They have preferred to abandon their villages until all the rodents had left of their own accord, or simply to lift the roofs from their homes and trust to the sunlight to drive the rats away.

The larger the settlement and the more dangerous the epidemic, the more willingness has been encountered among the people to join in, or at least to tolerate, protective measures. Trained native workers in India and Pakistan have been invaluable in persuading their own people to admit the health and sanitation teams. Community-wide assaults against cholera-carrying rats have been conducted in such areas with marked success, as have mass attacks against malaria through regular spraying of the houses by the DDT squads.

Practically every country, however, retains its pet superstitions which continue to raise difficulties for the purveyors of modern medical techniques. Everywhere, it appears, mystic lore surrounds illness in almost any phase, and the local versions are replete with their own peculiar remedies. These folk cures are not always insidious. A certain proportion are soundly based on healing properties of herbs or plants unfamiliar to outsiders, whose effectiveness more than once has astonished a modern practitioner. It was, in fact, a medicine man's feats in combatting malaria that led chemists to the discovery of quinine, as the source of his "magic." The trail of research thus opened is still being followed profitably. Unfortunately, however, a preponderance of remedies among primitive people are of the Mumbo Jumbo school, as apt to kill as to cure.

Near Lahore in Pakistan, a group of native girl students undertook to catalog an entire series of such beliefs as they heard them from the families in the region. For a Westerner, they make curious reading.

Their list was forwarded to New York by the head nurse at the midwifery school, an Englishwoman, who thought it might help to explain why contemporary medicine wins only reluctant acceptance in many parts of the world. It is now a part of an official agency file. The following excerpts are verbatim:

"Tuberculosis is thought to be due to a worm around the heart, which must be killed before the patient can recover. One method of treating it depends largely upon the magic number seven, and its multiples. Twenty-one grains of a special rice are put into a wooden cup with some juice of the *ak* plant (a succulent plant which secretes a milky fluid). This is left for seven days. Then the patient is instructed to pick out one grain a day with a needle and to swallow it, early in the morning, for twenty-one days. The rice grains will go straight to the worm, and poison it.

"Snake bite. The limb should be tied above the bite, and the *mullah* (local priest) sent for to offer prayers. The patient must be given milk, *ghee* (an oil obtained from buffalo milk) and pepper to drink, with the intention of causing nausea and getting the poison out of the body.

"Mad dog bite. Local applications of crushed red chilies, *surma* (eyeblack) and *haidi*, bandaged into place.

"Severe skin eruptions. Ash mixed with cow dung is applied to the skin.

"Boils and abscesses. A jar is heated by burning dung inside it. It is then placed while quite hot, on the affected area. After a few minutes it is removed, and the bulging area is lanced.

"Fits and madness. These are thought to be due to Jinns (bad spirits). They are treated by prayer and exorcism. The Jinns can be smoked out by burning cotton under the nose of the afflicted person. The Jinn is caught in a clay jar or a bottle (in which it drowns) and is buried in the graveyard. The person who buries it must on no account look back as he leaves.

"Bronchitis. Buffalo milk containing a drop of ammonia is boiled over a lamp—not over a fire. After skimming, the cream is given to the child.

"Tonsillitis and sore throat. Soot, surma and alum are ground together and applied to the inflamed membrane with the finger. Or, alum is fried and applied as a poultice to the throat.

"Discharging eyes. Opium, alum and butter are cooked together until dry, then crushed to powder. This is applied locally.

"Scrapes and bruises. A black cloth is burned. The ash is mixed with oil and applied to the sore spot."

The same group of Pakistani girls provided another list of customs and beliefs applying specifically to the expectant mothers attending their clinic, or whom they visited in their homes. Selections made at random from this document read:

"The head of the newborn (boy) is shaved at the fifth day, because the hair is thought to be the heritage of women, and unclean.

"We steal the hair of the newborn, burn it, mix the ash with water and drink, to make sure that we will have more children. A mother whose baby's hair has been stolen will not have any more children.

"The hair of the newborn has charm value, and is kept carefully. It is carried on special occasions to bring luck, as when a member of the family has to attend a court case.

"To avoid getting moon-struck, an expectant mother must never sit down during an eclipse of the moon, or the baby will be born with a deformity.

"Village women will not report when labor pains start, for fear of driving them away, or of prolonging labor. Only when pains have become strong will they inform their own mothers, or their mothers-in-law. (This custom is widely observed. It has caused much concern to trained midwives, who seldom manage to arrive in the home before the baby does.)

"If labor is slow, a dried date flower which resembles a hand is put into water. It will open slowly and labor will progress. Such a date flower is sometimes brought from Mecca and kept for this purpose. There is a tradition that Mary the Mother of Jesus held such a flower when she was in labor.

"Mothers believe that the baby comes into the world with a letter from Allah on which is written twenty promises. At birth this letter is snatched from the baby's hand by Allah's messengers, before the evil winds of the world can contaminate it. So baby cries lustily, vainly waving its empty hands.

"If birth is slow, the mother's friends and relatives unlock everything in the room. All padlocks are taken off tin trunks, windows and doors are opened, and the women unbind their hair. A gun is fired. This will alarm the baby and he will then make his appearance.

"As protection against the evil eye, an expectant mother makes a habit of giving to the crows, one fourth of each *chappati* (a sort of pancake) she eats."

Along with their notations about superstitions and local "cures," the students set down a brief account of the types of spirits believed by the people to live in and around their villages. They explained that "Pari" were spirits of cordial disposition, who were always kind to good people unless they had been offended. The Pari like to live in gardens under plum or pomegranate trees, they related, and it is therefore important to keep the soil under these trees clean, or the spirits will be offended. There was an old woman in a nearby village who claimed that she had often seen spirits, and that they are most easily glimpsed on a Thursday night, from the roof—usually in the form of a flame shimmering over a wheat field.

"Our own students," the head nurse commented in forwarding this information, "light candles around the tree in our school compound on Thursday nights, to please the spirit who lives there. It is a good spirit."

In the Western Hemisphere, the Andean Indian practices rites based on his own conception of the supernatural world about him. To him, this universe has many spirits—of the earth, of the mountains, of springs, animals or plants. At times he performs ceremonies intended to stir them up, and at other times to placate them.

He is convinced that the quality of the harvest depends to a large extent on the offerings that have been made to the *auki* (spirits of the earth) or the *apu* (spirits of the mountains), or to the good will that has been won from the winds, the hail or the frost.

Physical health depends, he is sure, on the spirits that inhabit rocks or trees, as well as on unknown beings imbued with demons. In his strange blend of Christianity and paganism, he tries to keep constant watch over the hidden forces of nature.

His witch doctors enjoy great prestige in the community, and are feared for their powers. These are frequently derived from circumstances, such as an apparently miraculous survival after being struck by lightning. Such an individual is able, the Indian is confident, to conjure up the spirits of the mountain and to ask them to punish a person with sickness, or to cure him, as well as to take away his soul, leaving him to exist without one. Their charges for consultation are so prohibitive that their aid is invoked only in very serious cases.

Other ailments are treated for the Indian by a less formidable, more popular figure, the *mai c'a* or quack doctor. This man normally inquires about symptoms and then proceeds to diagnose by means of divination. For the purpose he uses coca leaves, grains of maize or a guinea pig—rubbing the patient with its body and then dissecting the animal with a view to deciding which organs are affected by the disease from which the human suffers.

His treatments are administered in the form of poultices, potions and baths, involving herbs, fruits, mineral or animal substances. They are invariably accompanied by incantations intended to instill utter faith on the part of the patient, and the quack skillfully manipulates the factors that are supposed to govern results, so that his reputation in any case—whether the patient recovers or doesn't—is not endangered.

Among these people it is a characteristic belief that medicines which may cure a white man may endanger an Indian, and vice versa. It is difficult to introduce new curative methods, or to coax the Indians to accept scientific remedies and medicaments. Even to gain access to them, it is essential for a physician to be thoroughly acquainted with all Indian ideas and customs. Otherwise, there is small hope of devising appropriate ways of gaining acceptance for recognized methods.

Taboos ancient and modern constitute but one of many impediments the World Health Organization and its experts encounter all over the world. Teamed with the trained physicians, chemists and laboratory technicians in many countries, they have been through floods, typhoons and earthquakes, as well as enduring heat, cold, wind, sand, and mountain and desert journeys as a matter of course. They are bringing new techniques, new equipment and new drugs into the isolated regions, and are winning friends and allies everywhere, teaching and training as they go, that the work may continue after they themselves have left the field to the qualified nationals.

The agency has been an official part of the United Nations since November, 1947. It has a membership of seventy-nine countries, plus three associate members, and a staff of 750 men and women. Its headquarters are in Geneva and its budget in 1953 was $8,485,095. Dr. M. G. Candau of Brazil was elected in July of 1953 as its Director General, succeeding Dr. Brock Chisholm of Canada.

Concern with public health being universal, industrially advanced countries are benefiting from WHO programs as consistently as those of retarded areas. Man travels fast these days, and passengers from Asian countries may well carry with them unwittingly to Rio de Janiero, Sydney, Australia, or New York, typhus or other germs picked up en route.

From its short-wave radio station in Geneva, the WHO beams three times daily, warnings of any incipient epidemics. They are monitored widely, and used to guide quarantine procedures. WHO also maintains an influenza research center in London, which has contributed materially to the understanding of the varied types and characteristics of this disease.

In October of 1952, WHO efforts brought into operation the first code of International Sanitary Regulations. They standardize for scores of participating nations, the previously haphazard statutes that so delayed travelers and hampered the movement of ships and cargoes. As a consequence, delays have been cut and passenger and freight movements expedited. Also in 1952, the agency published the first International Pharmacopeia (formulas for drugs). By reference to this volume, pharmacists everywhere are enabled to fill with precision, any doctor's prescription regardless of the country in which it was written.

Governments have been diligent in their co-operation with the WHO. Groups and individuals, less aware of its influence on the world's welfare, have been more loath to relinquish their pet taboos and to permit medical science to do what it might for their physical and economic betterment.

But the wall erected through thousands of years of fears, prejudice and tradition is crumbling slowly. This is apparent in territories where during the brief life of the technical-assistance programs, medical science has made tremendous strides against such killers as malaria, yaws or typhoid.

Oddly enough, one of the most potent instruments in reaching isolated populations has been the hypodermic needle. The fact that it inflicts pain in the process of curing has proved to be its strongest recommendation among the more primitive populations. Unless the patient winces, their philosophy runs, the medicine is not strong. Part of its influence, medical men explain, harks back to the days when smallpox was rife and vaccinations were forcibly given by foreign doctors to tribesmen in "colonial" areas, in their determination to check its spread. The memory of that triumph has lingered. In these days, even aborigines submit gladly to the needle's prick, confident that the pain will once more be followed by a mass cure.

Another circumstance that makes the needle acceptable to secluded groups is the fact that they lost faith years ago in any form of pill or powder. Quack practitioners had sold them so many false remedies in these forms that the disillusioned victims refuse to be lured further.

This widespread response to the needle has proved an unexpected boon, but the WHO teams are now struggling with a different set of reactions toward their ministrations. They have not yet figured out a way to acquaint thousands of their patients with the meaning of a whole category of equipment intended only for diagnosis, which the simpler folk suppose are cures in themselves.

There is for example, the stethoscope, the X-ray for testing tubercular chests, and even the rubber arm band for blood-pressure examination. It is flattering yet exasperating to the WHO men to discover that once they have poked or probed or tapped a patient with any of these routine instruments, their subject considers that he has been treated, and will be cured without more ado. Why should he return to a clinic for further attention? Complications naturally ensue when the illness persists, and particularly when it worsens.

The more conscientious a team member may be, the oftener he fatigues himself, chasing into the hills or along some faintly marked bypath of a road, pursuing a fugitive patient to his hut in a distant village to administer something more potent than a stethoscope or an X-ray film (positive) can accomplish.

More often than not, time and distance as well as the anonymity with which many populations surround their fellow beings, defeats him. The fact that most of the WHO teams regard such pursuits as part of the week's work explains in large measure the splendid record they have achieved, against some of the heaviest odds history has yet registered.

Against half a hundred types of illness and epidemic, their healings have totaled not thousands—but millions.

TWELVE

THE ALTIPLANO PEOPLE

LOST IN the mists that obscure the pre-Inca period, the origin of a hardy race of Indians still tenaciously surviving on the high plateaus of the Andes will probably always remain a mystery. Fifty years before the arrival of the Spanish conquistadors, the last of these wild, free tribes yielded their independence to invaders from the south, as the kingdom of Quito (now Ecuador) was absorbed into the Inca empire.

In the succeeding eras their history has been one long tragedy of servitude and exploitation; of admixtures of new races, cultures and religions; and of strict repression of economic, social and educational opportunity. Now after 500 years, a generation that is coming more and more to abhor waste of resources—whether human or natural—is on the verge of doing something constructive about these reserved and lonely people. Plans formed after a long period of perplexity are on the brink of realization.

If they succeed, a glowing chapter will have been written into the history of social rehabilitation, and the world will applaud a gallant enterprise in human relations. Yet the findings of an international mission team sent to explore what could be done and how to do it most effectively, reveal the barriers that time, climate and segregation have built up among the Indians themselves.

For these people are of today, but live in the past to an extent that baffles the contemporary mind. Up on their lofty, wind-swept peaks and plains the majority eke out a substandard existence as a race apart, wearing the garb and speaking the tongues of their ancestors. Long and bitter experience has made them distrustful, hard to cultivate, resistant to change. A weaker group would have succumbed generations ago. Spanish rule is only a memory, and of the Incas, mere grandiose traces remain. The Indians, on the contrary, not only have outlived their subjugators but are gradually reverting to their own pure racial types, submerging all remnants of infusions of alien characteristics.

A certain proportion of them own a few acres—worn-out, infertile soil that stubbornly resists their patient efforts to cultivate it with their primitive tools, or level pasture land that must be reserved for their rangy herds of cattle, sheep or llama. They have for their own ground an attachment so exrtaordinarily deep and vital that it dominates their lives. Farther down the slopes lie semitropical, verdant valleys they might have for the taking, where crops could be raised easily and in abundance. The governments are eager to convey the titles, but the Indians will not budge from their hereditary holdings, and these rich farmlands go begging.

There are sound reasons for the Indians' rejection. They have been displaced before on alluring pretexts, only to find themselves shorn of their property and forced into peonage. Then too, these lower, lusher valleys are not always located within sight of the snow-crowned peaks they love as they love life itself. To banish an Indian from his mountain heights is to expose him to homesickness of the most virulent type.

Above all, to bring him down abruptly from the rarefied atmosphere in which his people have dwelt for centuries involves a transition he is physically incapable of making. Experience has proved that when they descend into humid coastal areas from their colonies—situated as high as 16,000 feet above sea level—Indians quickly acquire respiratory diseases such as pulmonary tuberculosis, to which they are apparently impervious in their accustomed altitudes.

This susceptibility was commonly recognized as a hazard for the subordinate race, during both Inca and Spanish supremacy. In both instances, when groups of Indians were transferred temporarily to low altitudes as workers on some project, two months was accepted as a maximum safety limit, before they were rotated back to their homes. Under the Spaniards an official decree provided stiff punishment for infringement of this regulation. And the Incas utilized the *yungas* (forest zones) as penal camps.

The reaction of the Indian population to the warmer, heavier air of the lowlands approximates the wilting effect of tropic heat on Arctic vegetation. They breathe with difficulty, suffer digestive upsets and can work only with unusual effort that quickly dissipates their energies.

Whereas in their own environment many Indians do heavy work, especially mining, they would almost certainly be decimated if compelled to perform such tasks at low altitudes. Adjustment would require caution and a long period of time, with constant attention to the physical condition of the people.

In their homeland nature has mingled oddly some features of weather conditions of both equatorial and Arctic regions. At points above 10,000 feet they live in an extremely dry, cold climate of a glacial type, yet although in the shade it is always chilly, the rays of the southern sun bring high temperatures during the day. Between the extremes of day-time and nighttime temperatures there is a sharp divergence. And since it has a strong influence on the living organism, the thinness of air on the high plateaus—sometimes equivalent to those of Tibet—is especially significant.

When in June of 1952 a United Nations team under Professor Ernest Beaglehole of New Zealand came into the plateau country for the Altiplano survey, members of the group found themselves experiencing—for opposite reasons—the same acute bodily discomforts that attack the Indians when they desert their heights. The decrease in oxygen content of the atmosphere brought on seizures of dizziness and digestive disturbances for the mission men. Fatigue came quickly. Aggravated by the incessant winds and the keenness of the cold, it forced them to retreat at intervals down the mountains, for a few days of recuperation. Despite this ordeal, their study was finished within six months.

One of its unanimous findings was that efforts to raise the living standards of the people should be made initially on their own lands, and under conditions to which they are inured. If a mass shift of the population develops later to-ward the lower valleys, it should find its stimulus among the people themselves, because they have come to recognize the advantages of easier living, in new surroundings. Some of them might be coaxed now to take up claims, the mission group realized, but they would drift back just as easily, for conditions could not be called ideal unless Indian skills were improved beforehand, through practice in their familiar locales.

The logic of this argument is conceded by the prime movers in the scheme to rehabilitate the Altiplano Indians. They are the three governments—Ecuador, Bolivia and Peru—of which these people are citizens. These governments have accepted the problem as a regional one. The decision to join in its solution led naturally to an appeal to the United Nations technical assistance program, which is ideally adapted to the role of co-ordinator. As the operating hub, the TA can tap the staffs of each agency for the appropriate technicians, and can also serve as a clearing-house on problems that would be formidable under unilateral administration.

Responsibility for formulating and steering the project fell to the International Labor Organization as a matter of course. As early as 1946, ILO's special competence for the task was conceded during an Inter-American Indian Congress at Mexico City, where its representatives first directed attention to the "problems of indigenous labor." At Cuzco, Peru, in July of 1946, the same congress voted to empower the ILO to organize a co-operative program among the appropriate agencies, to aid the Altiplano Indians toward integration into the working forces of their respective countries.

By January of 1951 the definitive stage was reached. At La Paz, Bolivia, an ILO committee of experts framed recommendations for a joint field-working party, to make basic studies on which a wide program of reconstruction should be planned. (This became the Andean Indian Mission, headed by Professor Beaglehole.) Priority should be given, it was suggested, to "those countries or regions in which the indigenous populations represent a high proportion of the total population."

Clear preference was established by this phrase for Bolivia, Peru and Ecuador, all of whom were poised to translate into reality their growing urge toward lifting the status of their Indians. Of their combined populations of 14,500,000, approximately 10,000,000 live in the Andean region—including some 6,600,000 Indians.

The term "Indian" is of necessity loosely applied. It covers a heterogenous group including people of differing tribes and ancestry, often divergent in their economic and social status as well as in their lingual and cultural backgrounds. Some have a proportion of Spanish blood and others have Inca heritage. They cannot even be designated by area, for many large landowners of the Altiplano trace their families proudly and clearly back to the conquistadors.

In fact, the single common denominator distinguishing the "Indians" may be said to be their inferior economic and social status and their universal plight. Nevertheless they reflect broadly similar ethnic traits and ways of life. And their symptoms of distress are rooted in almost identical conditions, regardless of locality.

They are to a great extent agriculturists. In the highlands

of Bolivia and of Peru, where there are tin mines and others bearing valuable minerals, groups of miners are concentrated numbering respectively about 60,000 and 39,000. There is also a scattering of semiskilled laborers—stonemasons, carpenters and makers of tile or of adobe bricks. Only a fraction of them earn more than a subsistence income.

Sturdy of physique for the most part, they show the usual effects of poor food badly prepared under unhygienic circumstances. Their dental deficiencies are numerous and neglected, and malnutrition has been evident among them for years, with its accompanying ailments. Their clothing is usually hand-woven of Indian design, frequently in the bright colors they have loved since colonial days, although contact with non-Indian groups has led to the adoption in some areas of cheap types of European garb. Often they go barefoot, and Indian feet are almost incredibly tough on the rocky soil. Some wear sandals, formerly made of rawhide but more often now fashioned of old automobile tires.

Their family life is extraordinarily close, extending to an embrace of godchildren as well as blood relatives. Except for an occasional *fiesta*, it is marked by almost constant labor, including that of even the younger sons and daughters. Each has his or her allotted chores either in the fields with the father, or around the house with the mother. Playtime for small Indians is regarded as not only unnecessary but frivolous, and from the age of five or six, they carry their minor responsibilities seriously, as they are taught.

Shunning their white neighbors even as they are shunned, Indians of the Altiplano frequently flee before the approach of anyone not of their caste. Yet among their own they are disposed to be frank and cordial and even gay, enjoying a joke or a prank the more because of the bleakness of their daily life. On the rare occasions when they can celebrate they do it thoroughly, forgetting for the time being the more difficult aspects of the land they inhabit.

The Altiplano itself is vast in scope and rugged in character. It extends roughly 2,000 miles from north to south—from Ecuador to southern Bolivia—and comprises a long cleft in the Andes. Here and there it is broken by mountainous knots which produce a series of high-walled and isolated valleys wherein Indians have huddled for generations. It varies in width from 100 to 400 miles, and in height from 7,500 to 16,250 feet.

The rivers, leaping and cascading at precipitous speeds, drain for the most part to the east, flowing into the Amazon or Plata basins. A few course westward to the Pacific or into Titicaca, which at 13,000 feet is the highest of the world's large lakes. In the latter area is concentrated one of the most sizable of the Indian population blocs, due to the abundant rainfall and the moderating influence the lake has on the temperatures. Some 600,000 Aymarans living there maintain themselves through agriculture, despite a density of population the more barren lands of the usual colony would be unable to sustain.

For Indians generally the paramount difficulty has been to wrest a living from the land for their families and their herds. Speaking mainly two ancient languages, Aymara and Quechua, they have been segregated through their illiteracy and their ignorance of Spanish, as well as by social antipathies that have endured for years.

On either side of these social barriers, dislike has been coupled with fear, except for a few cases where a deep attachment and real affection exist between certain Indians and their white neighbors. Resentment of their social ostracism is blended in Indian minds with fear of further discriminations, and of the laws they do not understand. Among non-Indians there is fear of drunken Indians—because so many turn to alcohol as a palliative for their deprivations. There is fear of contagion, due to Indian disregard for cleanliness and sanitation. And there is also fear of those who chew the coca leaf which grows so abundantly on the Altiplano, because it is widely believed that the leaf causes mental and physical degeneration.

Authorities disagree as to whether this custom constitutes addiction to a habit-forming drug. That it dulls mental faculties, as well as easing hunger among people whose rations are too short for heavy labor, is readily admitted. It is agreed that it would disappear gradually if the Indian diet could be increased and balanced.

The broad program of rehabilitation outlined by the Andean Indian mission under TA auspices is designed to do not only that, but much more. It is scaled to last five years, at an approximate cost of $200,000 annually, rising in 1955—the peak year—to $500,000, then decreasing as it becomes self-sustaining. The major share of this investment would be supplied by the governments co-operating in the plan.

At a slow but fairly steady pace, it envisages many changes in the agricultural field, through the help of the Food and Agriculture Organization. Fertilizers would be introduced to revitalize the soil through replacement especially of its phosphorous deficiencies. New seeds would be obtained, better adapted to the climate, and the overgrazed pasture lands replanted with native grasses. More modern techniques of farming would be taught to the Indians gradually—or retaught, because they have forgotten old skills learned from the Incas, such as terracing for better crops. And as the farmers learned to handle them, more efficient tools would be provided.

For the herdsmen, the FAO veterinarians would bring vaccines to combat animal diseases, and would introduce cross-breeding and selective breeding to improve the types of cows and sheep, aiming at development of sturdier and healthier strains. Research would be launched on the possibilities in crossing and breeding the alpaca and the llama, since the latter plays an important part in the Indian economy, as a beast of burden. The survey team also pointed out that the vicuña—living in a wild state at this altitude—could be domesticated and may have excellent revenue-producing potentialities because of its famous soft, thick wool.

Potatoes, wheat, barley, rye and oats all are grown on the Altiplano, but with indifferent success. Development of larger and finer yields would necessitate not only hybridization and better seeds, but newer methods of planting and harvesting. The ancient sickle is used now to reap the grain, threshing is handled by the treading of oxen, donkeys or mules, and winnowing is done by the wind, as it has been for centuries. Mechanization is impractical. Most commercial implements are too large for Altiplano conditions, and the people are ill-equipped to use them or keep them in repair. But improved plows, potato diggers and grain binders are possible and would mean good returns through saving of time and labor.

Even before an agricultural revolution can take hold, two essential needs of the population must be met. They are closely interrelated—housing and health. The first is the function of the FAO and the second of the World Health Organization, but they dovetail so neatly that technicians of each hardly distinguish where one leaves off and the other begins. Until better types of shelter can be provided health will continue to suffer, and the prospective extension of the governmental medical services into the remote colonies will be seriously handicapped.

Present housing conditions are described thus in one section of the Andean Indian Mission's report:

"The dwellings vary not only with the climate but with the materials available. In Bolivia and Peru, within a single area (Lake Titicaca) there may be seen the most varied types of construction, due to the difference in materials, ranging from beaten earth and roots for both walls and roof, to a wooden framework and thatched or tile roof. In all cases the floor is of earth. The dwellings are unventilated and in most of them the inside is black with soot from the fire, which is nearly always on the floor.

"Very often the home consists of one or two rooms which serve for cooking, sleeping and also keeping small domestic animals (fowls and guinea pigs). The beds are either on the floor or on a platform of sticks and stones and mud, and consist of sheepskins and a few hand-woven blankets in varying conditions of wear and preservation—or the reverse. In Ecuador, although a large percentage of the houses are of this small type, they have a better appearance than the average in Bolivia and Peru and there are some—not many— with whitewashed roofs and wooden floors."

The basic problem in the stabilization and advancement of the Indians, however, is that of providing land for those who have none. For an Indian without land lacks more than the means of sustenance. He is without prestige or dignity in the eyes of his friends, his family or himself. He is a peon, condemned to the most menial of chores on one or another of the big estates, to whose owner he has bound himself in return for the privilege of grazing his few animals.

Often without any return in cash wages, he toils from dawn to dark for three or four days a week or even longer, watching the owner's herds, mending fences, chopping wood, milking, fetching water or running errands. He is tied to the hacienda, without leisure to work for himself, without security and without hope of change. He spends his life in stagnation, unable to take any step to expand his experience, his understanding or his abilities.

Even when he lives as a member of an Indian community owning land jointly, the constant subdividing of acreages to provide plots for his sons and his relatives frustrates his attempts to farm profitably. During 1951 a Peruvian studying the motivations of migrant workers in his own country, on behalf of the ILO, mentioned the acute shortage of arable land that has arisen through the steady increase of population and the continuous subdivision of property rights through inheritance. In some areas of the high plateaus, he stated, especially in Cuzco, Puno and Apurimac, the fragmentation of holdings has reached such incredible proportions that "allotments are calculated in terms of furrows." The practice, he added, amounted to "an atomization of property rights."

"The land thus fragmented no longer fulfills its economic and social function," the researcher declared. "It has become merely a source of embittered boundary disputes."

Further complicating the agricultural picture is the tendency to sow the fields nearest to the dwellings until they are exhausted, and to use the farther ones for grazing, without rotation.

On the large estates—usually the most productive land in the region—the same routine is followed, only a small portion of the acreage nearest the houses being used for crops.

Thus, while the Indian lands grow more and more crowded and less and less productive, great stretches of the haciendas are left untilled and untrodden, and imbalances mount. The governments concerned are soberly aware of this drag on their separate economies. For political and social reasons, redistribution is not always possible, but plans are afoot in some parts of the Andes for expropriation of portions of larger holdings, and for resettlement of groups of Indians on such lands.

Discouraging as the outlook seems at present because of the lack of training or skills among the most isolated of the Indian population, we know that an appreciable number will respond readily to such a program.

Cheerful proof of this fact lies in the voluntary efforts the

Indians have made over a long interval, to help themselves.

Of these ventures, the oldest and probably most important is the Muquiyauyu colony in the Mantaro Valley in Peru. It is a settlement of about 4,000 Quechua-speaking people in the department of Junin, east of Lima, and comprises a self-governing unit that has been in existence more than seventy years, on a co-operative basis. Some of the younger members used to leave for work in the mines at Oroya, Morococha and Cerro de Pasco. Later land was rented from the Church and has been farmed communally, returning a moderate profit.

As long as forty years ago these Indians took the surprising initiative of building their own hydroelectric station, financing it with their farm profits. For decades the group has sold electric current to adjacent villages, including the provincial capital of Jauja. From this income the colony at one time provided education at a secondary school and university for its more promising children. Several were trained as doctors, lawyers and schoolteachers, in the expectation that the community would benefit. These hopes were shattered when none of the young professionals returned as a resident, and the program was regretfully abandoned.

The government has established several services in the region. There is a hospital, a college, an agricultural and stock-breeding experimental station and a health center. The community now owns a sawmill and a leather factory, and—in conjunction with the owner of a neighboring estate —is in the process of installing a small woolen spinning plant, with modern machinery imported from Germany. Its housing and its water supply are still far from satisfactory, and the returns from farming and forestry are too meager for normal family requirement. Yet Muquiyauyu is considered by the Andean Indian Mission team as an ideal "anchor project" from which to extend their attempts to improve conditions throughout the area.

Outside assistance would, at this stage, be a genuine tonic. Farm experts from the Extension Training Center at Lima could be brought in to advise the population—of whom ninety per cent depend on agriculture for their livelihood. In the colony the training of future leaders could be carried out concurrently with programs for improvement of the soil, the cattle and farming techniques. Advanced instruction in animal husbandry could be supplied to the same men at the Kcaira experimental station near Cuzco. Afterward the trainees could be stationed at various points, with proper equipment, to disseminate the knowledge as widely as possible among their own people.

In Bolivia the Beaglehole party encountered the most successfully planned and directed scheme in the Andean area, for promoting integration of the aborigines into the national life. This was the Huata-Jaca settlement on the banks of Lake Titicaca, consisting of estates acquired in 1914 by Antonio Cherioto, an Italian who had been selected to carry out the terms of a will left by Pinio Hall. Hall's intention had been to aid the Indians through a variation of the type of program now in prospect under United Nations supervision. Relatively little was done, however, until the property was taken over some years later by a mission of the Canadian Baptist Church.

The missionaries began by cultivating the friendship and

good will of the Indians. With this background of confidence established, they began slowly to demonstrate new ways of building low-cost houses, with satisfactory hygiene and conveniences suited to Indian requirements. Next they undertook to help the people obtain a supply of pure water and some better tools, and finally to make an equitable division of the estate, retaining a portion for the mission and making over the remainder to the Indians who had formerly worked on the land as peons.

Each of the new plots became the possession of the smallholder only after he had built a house according to models and plans provided by the missionaries—who also helped him to get the materials, loaned him the tools and even pitched in with their own hands to speed its construction. Later the mission men formed a co-operative among the consumers, at which they could buy sugar, rice and other commodities they did not raise themselves. A representative of the mission admitted that only after twenty years and patiently repeated demonstration and instruction, have appreciable results been obtained.

Today the houses in the Huata-Jaca center are noticeably better than those in nearby villages. Members of the Beaglehole team inspected one of these homes and reported that it consisted of five rooms, well plastered and oil painted, with large glass windows and wooden floors. The interior was very clean. Furnishings included a clothes cupboard, two metal bedsteads and cradles and a writing table covered with a cloth of native weave, at which a boy was busy on his homework. Paraffin lamps gave illumination.

The quality of the Indian diet at Huata-Jaca has been

much improved through the foods obtainable at the co-operative, and there has been a general increase in agricultural production in the community. Most of the adults still speak only the Aymaran language, but a good percentage of the children are in school and attendance is regular. The curriculum begins in the native tongue, and becomes bilingual as Spanish is added later.

The UN men noticed that attempts had been made in the surrounding countryside to imitate the Huata-Jaca houses for a radius of about ten miles, but with only indifferent effectiveness. Yet the fact that it was tried at all indicated that the spirit of self-improvement was present, and that other Bolivian Indians as well would make the effort to lift their standards, if technical assistance were offered.

In southeastern Peru, where land shortages are most extreme, community Indians from Sandia crossed the mountains of their own volition some years ago, and set up colonies at San Carlos, at Sina and in the lower Tambopata Valley, at medium altitudes and in cool-temperate climates. Their unusual migration was in the nature of an escape from this badly overpopulated region, and this enterprise has since been given official recognition by the Peruvian government.

Ties with the home region have been retained by the settlers. Markets have been organized for their products, and are well attended by the people of the neighboring villages.

Possibly because of the initiative of these groups, the Peruvian government is anxious to explore the potentialities of a much more extensive colonization of the Tambopata Valley. If it can be opened up, it will materially relieve the high density of population in the province of Puno, where the land available to Indians is insufficient to feed them. The TA mission team approved the suggestion and has recommended that an FAO expert be assigned to study the possibilities of growing such crops as tea, coffee, cacao, rubber, bananas and other fruits in this subtropical to tropical area.

An affirmative report by the FAO man would mean that the migrants—given access to markets—would be able to raise enough food for themselves from the start, and also realize some cash income. The study is expected also to indicate the minimum acreage each family would need in the valley to raise its livestock.

With its eyes on the future and the possible desire of many more Indians to migrate to greener pastures, the TA team has designated several centers which should be used as a focal point for attracting such families and helping them to orient themselves.

An example is the Jésus de Machaca-Tiahuanacu estate in Bolivia, on the shore of Lake Titicaca. It consists of four haciendas with a total area of 7,417 hectares, of which only 2,811 are cultivated. Only about one hundred *coloños* and their families are living there, but 600 families could be readily accommodated. The TA men have recommended that four FAO experts should be sent to Tiahuanacu to advise on pasture management and crop production, animal husbandry, small handicrafts and better tools. Each would remain for two years and would participate in organizing the project.

In a breakdown of the plans submitted for this development, it has been calculated that new homes of adobe could be erected at a cost of only about $40 per house, provided the settlers themselves made the bricks and did the construction work.

FAO men assigned to the Tiahuanacu estates can easily divide their time between this and a second rehabilitation center in the Vacas Valley. Here, some 600 Indian farmers are waging a losing fight to grow crops and cattle, while production decreases annually. If statistics are accurate, the volume has dropped almost seventy-five per cent within ten years.

The reasons for the slump are fairly obvious. The Vacas region is made up of four valleys at altitudes of 10,000 to 12,000 feet, surrounded by mountain ridges of nearly 15,000 feet. The hills have been denuded by the population through cutting of the forests for fuel, by overgrazing and by burning the grassy slopes. Agricultural methods are poor, equipment is primitive, inferior seed is sown and the land is badly overstocked and overused. With practically no good pastures left, twenty to thirty head of sheep are kept per hectare, and during drought periods many die from starvation. The yield of field crops is low although every square meter is cultivated, and the Indians are mere subsistence farmers.

Selected seed and more modern methods could increase production considerably, the Andean Indian Mission men declared. There is also a good possibility of culling and improving the livestock through the usual routines of selection, cross-breeding and proper feeding. And the region has four lagoons which are fed by rainwater and which could be used for irrigation and for hydroelectric power.

How far the recommendations of the Beaglehole party

can be implemented depends mainly upon the funds that can be made available in this as in other of the area programs, from the participating governments and from ETAP itself. The ILO has plunged into the tasks as quickly as possible and to the widest extent for which personnel and funds could be amassed.

Organization of the job was begun in the autumn of 1953, with a recruitment program for the various experts listed as necessary by the Andean Indian Mission. Some members of the staff are now under contract and on their way to the Andes.

As the most direct channel to their objectives, this vanguard of technicians will launch their activities from under the sheltering wing of some of the centers and organizations already established among the Indians, whose collaboration will be invaluable and who can sponsor them among their Indian friends and acquaintances. They will make use of not only the national governmental institutions, but also all training schools and welfare offices maintained by international associations or foundations.

One of the natural springboards for the expanded operations will be the development of Indian handicrafts, which promise relatively quick returns to the workers and the opportunity to go on from there to other types of training. Local conditions will dictate the program in many cases, as in Otavalo, Ecuador, whose people by consensus possess the highest degree of skills of any of the Andean Indians.

Otavalo lies about seventy miles north of Quito in the province of Imbabura. It has about 10,000 inhabitants and its residents are more distinctively landowners than other mountain Indians of that country. The group is especially adept in wool spinning, dyeing and weaving, ceramics, embroidery, manufacture of felt hats and the spinning and weaving of sisal fibers, but their tools are inferior and their designs, despite their popularity with tourists, lack the flair that would permit competition with European or other products.

Months ago the Institute of Inter-American Affairs sent technicians to Otavalo to advise these craftworkers on improvements in their designs and finishes, to widen the market for them, and afford the possibility of additional income.

Identical programs can be opened up, the ILO believes, among other Indian tribes whose traditional pottery and weaving have their own attractiveness, even though they cannot rival the artistic colors and gay designs achieved by the Otavalo colony. The potential is there, and the ILO is prepared to invest time, funds and personnel in cultivating it.

In this field the sponsoring agency has the advantage of long experience. The ILO is the only one of the specialized agencies of the United Nations that was taken over from the League of Nations—of which it was a unit for a number of years—and many of its present staff acquired their backgrounds through that continuity. It is dedicated to the improvement of relations between employers and employees. Within that orbit it has accomplished much toward raising efficiency among workers, as well as in improving conditions of employment.

Organized in 1919, the ILO embraces representatives of government, labor and management, all of whom have their places on its governing board, headed at present by David A. Morse as director-general. Its headquarters are in Geneva, and sixty-nine nations hold membership. The permanent staff numbers 700 men and women, many of whom are familiar with conditions in half a dozen countries. The annual budget in 1953 was $6,223,368, out of which, as usual, a substantial sum was spent on scholarships and fellowships. Many of these were exchange fellowships. Through them, potential leaders were sent to other countries for a period of months, and brought back to their home factories not only the know-how they acquired in stipulated lines of production or manufacture, but also the "feel" of their neighboring lands and an understanding of the political, social and civic life of their temporary co-workers.

Group visits of selected workers have been organized during the last few years under ILO sponsorship, for briefer travels into adjacent countries, with excellent results. The participants are given opportunities to talk with both employers and employed in their own and related occupations, to visit vocational-training schools, and to explore other aspects of life that interest them. The benefits of these tours have been undeniable.

In the Andean Indian rehabilitation project the ILO has tackled the vastest and toughest chore of its thirty-five years of existence. Luckily, its staff has behind it a fulsome record of success in grappling with major obstacles. Instead of recoiling from the prospect, the agency that has learned how to retreat temporarily but not to yield, is approaching the crucial test in Latin America with the air of a challenger confronting the champ, realizing that he is going to take plenty of punishment but cocksure of victory when the final gong clangs.

THIRTEEN

A TEST CASE -
THE REMODELING
OF A NATION

BOLIVIA

BOLIVIANS SOMETIMES say of their country that it is "a beggar seated on a chair of gold." By this they mean that if the wealth of minerals and metals embedded in their native earth could be mined and marketed properly, their destitute masses would stand forth as one of the richest of the world's populations. That time is not yet—nor even dimly discernible.

Only a single phase of their national El Dorado has ever been adequately tapped. The tin mines of the Altiplano have produced some of the greatest fortunes of modern eras—all but a fraction of which have gone to swell the coffers of a restricted group comprising only about fifteen per cent of the people. The rest were peons, teetering perilously and constantly on the ragged edge of starvation. No middle class has ever existed there.

Latin tempers run hot, and those who have suffered have never been disposed to endure in silence. Political ferment

253

has boiled unceasingly in this land of pinnacles and abysses—social as well as geographic. Its history has been an unbroken succession of uprisings and bloodlettings, and the overthrow of administrations by new ones that were in turn overthrown.

Since 1825, when Simon Bolivar and Antonio José de Sucre liberated that part of South America from Spanish rule and made it a nation, Bolivia has experienced no less than 180 revolutions. Only ten governments have succeeded peacefully to power. Its presidents have resigned under pressure, fled into exile or expired violently in one of its seething rebellions.

As late as 1946, President Gualberto Villaroel, dying in his palace from gunshot wounds, was seized by the attackers and hurled from the balcony to instant death among the insurgents below. His body was then hung for two days from a lamppost nearby, which is still pointed out to wide-eyed tourists from more tranquil regions.

Into this political and economic chaos the United Nations in 1950 sent a survey mission, to find out what might be done to bring stability and order to the tortured country. Mamerto Urriolagoitia at that time occupied the uneasy post of chief executive, but the appeal he had directed to the newly formed world organization had more than partisan endorsement. Leaders of all factions that honestly desired a brighter future for their nation were weary of the futile struggle. Still at odds on many matters, they were at one in acceptance of the fundamental philosophy, that political steadiness could be brought about only on the basis of economic soundness.

For a year, while the situation mercifully remained in

status quo, the five-man mission compiled its data and decided what might be done, and how, to rescue the ailing economy. At the head of the mission was Hugh Keenleyside of Canada, Director-General of the Technical Assistance Administration, who wrote the final, detailed report.

It called for a five-year program of energetic work under the direction of the government, supervised by a United Nations staff of seven experts and fifteen technical consultants. It pointed out that the Bolivians had for too long "put all their eggs into one tin pail"—that diversification was a crying need. Seventy per cent of the country's exports had consisted of tin ore, and any break in prices on the world market had brought shuddering repercussions throughout the nation.

The report therefore envisioned improvements in the fields of public administration, finance and social welfare; road construction and development of hydroelectric power; and exploitation of the extensive deposits of silver and gold, zinc, copper, lead, antimony and wolfram. Geological surveys were needed, agriculture should be advanced and small industries fostered.

Over several more months the findings were studied carefully, both by United Nations officials and by Bolivian executives in the capital at La Paz, where storm clouds were gathering once more over the political scene, as elections neared. They were held May 15, 1951. Half a dozen parties had slates of candidates on the ballots. No single contender won a clear majority, but Victor Paz Estenssoro of the National Revolutionary Movement garnered forty-five per cent of the votes, under astonishing circumstances.

Paz Estenssoro himself was in exile in Argentina—more than 3,000 miles away. He had served as minister of finance under Villaroel, and had escaped the fury of the mob that had cut down the president even while an airplane waited with motors idling, to fly him to safety. Now it was Urriolagoitia's turn to flee his homeland. He did so while the electorate clamored for the return of Paz Estenssoro, and rival parties disputed the legitimacy of his claim to office.

On May 16th the predicament was resolved in typical Bolivian fashion. A military *junta* of ten men led by General Hugo Ballivian seized power, announcing that it would serve temporarily, until the issue could be settled through new presidential elections.

The country settled back into relative calm. And in October of 1951, General Ballivian signed the five-year contract with ETAP. For the first time, the United Nations was undertaking to assist a country in all aspects of its economy, rather than after a patchwork pattern that concentrated on the needier branches alone. Recruiting for experts was begun, and presently they began to arrive in La Paz.

Under another unique provision of the contract, these men were enrolled as civil servants of the government they were aiding, and drew their salaries from the national treasury. For the duration of their two-year assignments they became employees of the several ministries in which they served as advisers—but without affecting their citizenship in their homelands. By February of 1952 most of them were immersed in their several projects.

Two months later the lid again blew off the Bolivian

caldron, and blood was shed freely as Ballivian and his associates of the *junta* vanished from the scene. Paz Estenssoro returned triumphantly to power in the revolution led by Hernan Siles Zuazo on his behalf. In the Secretariat building in New York, United Nations executives pored over the fragmentary bulletins arriving from the scene, waiting anxiously for word about the safety of their emissaries, the technical consultants and the experts they had commissioned. The mission at that time was under the direction of Dr. Carter Goodrich of Columbia University, who had reached La Paz less than a week earlier, for a year's stay.

A few days later Bolivia had subsided as usual after its periodic outburst. The technicians were all safe. The bodies of 450 victims were interred and the hospitals were treating 1,750 of the injured. Paz Estenssoro, only thirty-seven years old, occupied the presidential palace.

At the start, his administration could hardly have been less auspicious. On the basis of letters discovered by the Allied occupation forces in Germany after the capitulation, this former professor of economics was accused, especially in the United States, of having collaborated with Nazi and Fascist elements during the war. Paz Estenssoro himself repeatedly protested that these charges were untrue and the documents forgeries. He was willing and even anxious to establish and maintain good relations with Washington.

In other quarters he was denounced—rather inconsistently—as being sympathetic to Communist policies and philosophies. The Communists themselves certainly shared these views and lent him their enthusiastic support.

Making the best of what it considered a bad business,

nevertheless demanding above all the speediest possible relief of the population, the United States accepted President Paz Estenssoro on trial and advanced him a loan of $9,000,-000. Meanwhile his government went into conference with Dr. Goodrich about the technical assistance contract. It was essential and must be continued, they decided, but revisions would be necessary. Again it came under study and over additional months was altered in various respects, none of which reduced its importance to Bolivia.

A second signing ceremony took place in May of 1953, with stipulations that the period covered would remain fixed—five years dating from the original 1951 agreement was still the target.

In the interim Paz Estenssoro's administration had registered many and vital changes. He had installed a new cabinet, had weathered the inevitable financial crisis with the earnest help of the United Nations experts, had decreed nationalization of the tin mines and, after months of study, had even gratified the United States by arranging for compensation for the former owners. The State Department in Washington, relying upon advice from its representatives in La Paz, announced publicly that during the preceding three months the Bolivian president had brought his country greater stability than in the entire interval since he assumed the helm, and that it would be pleased to advance his government another loan—this time for $15,000,000.

At this point the Communist party, which had tried hard to maintain as much confusion as possible in the country, turned on Paz Estenssoro and denounced him as an enemy of the people. Its press, that had commended him so long, now vigorously attacked him.

This characteristic reversal of tactics did not appear to dismay the administration. It proceeded to initiate one of the most historic movements in the country's history— agrarian reform, proclaimed late in 1953.

Dr. Walter Guevara Arze, Bolivia's minister of foreign affairs, visited United Nations headquarters just before the Christmas holidays last year, discussing the implications gravely with executives there and with representatives of the international press. It meant, he explained, that for the first time, nearly 2,500,000 peons who had lived in virtual slavery for centuries had been emancipated, to live as free men. Under the traditional hacienda system, the owners had possessed all rights to their labor and were able to employ them without pay if they wished. Many had never availed themselves of the power and had paid at least some small wages. Now, under the law, they were compelled to do so.

"One cannot banish so deeply implanted a practice merely by legislation," Dr. Arze acknowledged. "It will be years before it is even understood among large numbers of these illiterate and impoverished people. But whether they know it or not, they now are free and the system of peonage is illegal. Eventually they will get land to work for themselves, and peonage will disappear, gradually but certainly."

One of the major improvements the present technical-assistance program already has brought, Dr. Arze reported, is the establishment of a great sugar mill under construction near Santa Cruz, scheduled to go into operation in 1955. The United Nations expert who was sent to help choose the site and plan the construction was Alexander Mackenzie, a Scottish engineer who had worked for twenty-five years in the sugar industry, in Great Britain, Brazil, India and Cuba. This mill will have a daily capacity of 100 tons of refined sugar, pressed from 1,000 tons of crushed cane, and will help materially to reduce the necessity for importing this commodity, consumption of which is estimated at 45,000 tons annually. Although the dampness of the atmosphere restricts operations to only 180 days every twelve months, prospects are that the mill will produce 10,000 tons during that period. The investment required was $2,500,000, made possible through the loans Bolivia had obtained.

Of all the potentialities of the little country, United Nations men are most dazzled by its unharnessed water resources, which could produce unlimited quantities of electric power if the funds were available to set up the power stations and the conducting lines. Torrents of mountain streams cascading down from awesome heights suggest the possibilities inherent in these sources of natural energy— sufficient to provide current not only for Bolivia itself but for adjacent areas.

The obstacles are almost as formidable. The heights and depths that must be scaled to install the power stations and the transit lines have made the development of such resources impracticable, until roads can be built over which to cart the construction materials and the great turbines and towers that must be installed. Some day in the future these minor Niagaras may be equipped to perform for the benefit of Bolivians and others. Now, as in past ages, they course merrily and freely on their separate ways.

Road building is in progress, however. It is a key project,

designed to unlock for development and settlement especially the Cochabamba Valley in the heart of the country, considered by Bolivians as their most fertile land. On the steep highways that lace the mountain passes, few vehicles are usable except four-ton trucks. Even they are able to make only approximately fifty to sixty miles per day, and require constant repair of their laboring motors to keep them operative.

As this book goes to press, a loan is being sought from the International Bank for Reconstruction and Development, to provide at least part of the hydroelectric power that is so badly needed for smelting operations at the tin mines. Formerly Bolivia shipped all her ore out of the country to be processed, because she lacks coal and oil that might be utilized for smelting. Now the construction work for the first large unit is under way, and the equipment is being transported with the greatest difficulty to the higher plateaus where it will ultimately make possible far greater profits from the nationalized mines.

Dr. Goodrich finished his stint in Bolivia and returned to his teaching duties in New York early in 1954. His place as director of the program was taken by Dr. Sune L. Carlson, who reported at La Paz in January of 1954.

At a snail's pace but with steadily greater momentum, the technical-assistance work in Bolivia goes forward. On the Rio Ibirisu, 100 miles from the nearest railroad at Cochabamba city, a power plant is planned from which it is intended to transmit current over long lines to the tin-mining town of Oruro, for the smelting process. Each short stretch of traversable road completed represents another forward step, making access possible to the agricultural land that lies unclaimed and uncultivated, or the mineral deposits awaiting the miner's pick or the transport truck.

These last few years have brought the franchise to every man and woman, literate or illiterate, among Bolivia's 3,-500,000 population. Previously ballots could be cast only by approximately 100,000—the favored few who could meet the prerequisite of property ownership, and who had for so long controlled the fate of their fellow countrymen.

Uncertainty still clouds the future. The threat of revolution still envelops the presidential palace. Paz Estenssoro is by no means firmly in the saddle as yet, and, in any case, his term is due to expire in 1957. Re-election under the constitution adopted in 1945 would not be possible until another six years had elapsed.

So the world waits and wonders about the fate of this initial test of United Nations ability to pull a backward and badgered nation out of its morass of inequality and poverty, up to its potential status of prosperity and stability.

The odds are long but not desperate. After all, a program of technical assistance that stood as solid as Gibraltar through two revolutions and three administrations cannot yet be counted out of the running. The race is with revolution, with Communist agitation, with famine and illiteracy and disease.

At the moment, the specialized agencies co-operating in Bolivia are neck and neck with their opponents, and giving no ground. The next few years will tell the story and indicate the winners.

POSTSCRIPT

PRESSTIME FOR this volume finds the United Nations technical assistance program once again under the imminent risk of collapse. Unhappily, a vote last month in the House of Representatives in Washington threatens to scuttle the prospect of smooth sailing in the future, after the financial stringencies the ETAP encountered in 1953.

Deadlines are inflexible, and the printer waits. Yet the only hopeful note that can be recorded at this juncture is that a partial rescue of the situation may be effected by the more amiably disposed Senate, through a compromise with the House on the pending legislation.

Recent developments began with an adverse recommendation by the Appropriations Committee of the House, against a proposed allocation of $17,958,000 for the United Nations program, up to June of 1955. When it came to the floor, it was upheld by an overwhelming vote.

Only then was it discovered that both actions stemmed from a misconception. Some Representatives had been deeply angered to learn that thirteen technicians assigned to handle projects in non-Communist countries, had come from "iron curtain" lands. United States contributions, the opponents argued, were obviously being misused to spread doctrines inimical to this nation, therefore the entire appropriation should be cancelled. And it was. In the hectic atmosphere of the closing days of a Congressional session, time was lacking for adequate appraisal.

Promptly thereafter, the thirteen were revealed as actual refugees from Communism, who had fled their homelands rather than live under totalitarian regimes. President Eisenhower among others, voiced his concern and his dismay at the treatment accorded an appropriation item he considered imperatively necessary. He was confident, he told a press conference, that the Senate would evaluate more accurately the importance of the matter, and would restore the appropriation.

To date this has not been done. Unofficial reports from the Senate-House conference are that the lower house may agree to an allocation of $9,958,000, which would cover only the commitment made to the program for the remainder of 1953, by the United States delegation to the United Nations. The remaining $8,000,000 appears doomed.

There is still the possibility that an attempt might be made early in 1955, to secure additional funds. But since the ETAP planners must operate on a long-term basis, and the next pledging conference will be held late in 1954, only a fortuitous shift of circumstances can apparently stave off another critical interval for the program that has leaned so heavily on United States support.

So heavily, in fact, that if it is withdrawn chances are slim indeed that the structure will survive.

Informed public figures in Washington and elsewhere, who realize the impact of the House decision and the extent of the damage already done, have asked incredulously,

"Are we who have done so much to make this program possible, going to walk out on it now—just when the USSR and its satellites have walked in?"

Time will tell. Wider understanding of what is involved, and deeper appreciation of what has been accomplished, if weighed against the alternative, could tip the balance. In this interlude of uncertainty—and later—it may be interesting to ponder the fact that the going price for a B-36 jet bomber, as quoted today by the United States Army, is $3,600,000. To a defense-minded nation, bombers are indispensable in this age, and we have acquired many. By comparison with rearmament costs, our expenditures for the stimulation of economic progress in underdeveloped countries have been modest. They too, however, constitute defense—against the capitulation of underprivileged populations to Communist infiltration. Even a minimal rise in standards of living bolsters the spirit as well as stiffening the spine.

An old Chinese proverb runs thus;

"If you plant for the years, plant grass. If you plant for the decades, plant trees. If you plant for the centuries, plant men!"

INDEX